CHINESE VILLAGE COOKBOOK

BY RHODA YEE
PHOTOGRAPHY BY SPAULDING TAYLOR

YERBA BUENA PRESS · SAN FRANCISCO · 1975

TO ALL LOVERS
OF
CHINESE FOOD

LONG LIVE THE WOK!

ISBN 0-912738-07-3

Library of Congress Card #75-18964
Printed in the United States of America
Copyright © 1975 by Yerba Buena Press
Published by Taylor & Ng — Yerba Buena Press
666 Howard Street
San Francisco, California 94105
    All Rights Reserved
    First Edition 2nd Printing

Distributed by Random House, Inc.
and in Canada by Random House of Canada, Ltd.
ISBN #394-73152-2

The Publisher wishes to thank Betty Kilich for reading and editing *Chinese Village Cookbook*.

ABOUT THE AUTHORESS

Rhoda Fong Yee was born in Canton, capital of Kwongtung province in Southern China. A good part of her childhood was spent in Loan Gon Doan, her father's village. It was her experience during this part of her childhood which inspired Rhoda to write *The Chinese Village Cookbook.*

At the age of twelve, Rhoda migrated to this country and settled in Sacramento, California. She learned the basics of Chinese cuisine from her mother, who is an excellent cook, having received training from several family chefs.

In 1962, three years after graduating from U.C. Berkeley, Rhoda married Paul Yee, who coincidentally shares her love and enthusiasm for Chinese food. Together, they have delighted their friends with scrumptious Chinese feasts in their home in Walnut Creek.

Rhoda began to give Chinese cooking instructions six years ago. Her expertise in the Chinese culinary art, the vivaciousness of her personality and her quick sense of humor create an uncanny ability to establish fast rapport with her audiences. Besides carrying a full teaching schedule, Rhoda presents numerous Chinese cooking lectures and demonstrations throughout California.

ABOUT THE PHOTOGRAPHER

Chinese Village Cookbook's photographer, Spaulding Taylor, was born in Buffalo, New York, in 1934. In 1959 he emigrated to San Francisco where he sought fine arts training in painting and ceramics at the San Francisco Art Institute. Mr. Taylor proceeded to establish a distinguished career in ceramics and ceramic design through a series of exhibits and one man shows. In 1960 he joined with Win Ng; together they developed Taylor & Ng, the San Francisco wholesale, retail, and publishing firm.

San Francisco and its Chinese traditions have long influenced Spaulding Taylor. Chinese food is one of his driving interests and specialties; combined with his abilities in photography, shooting *Chinese Village* was a natural and pleasurable endeavor. The *Chinese Village Cookbook* is Taylor's first on location photographic effort — recording and recreating the everyday human love affair with food: how it is prepared, where it comes from, how marvelous, intricate yet uncomplicated it can be. Spaulding Taylor's photographs are filled with fact, humanism, and fancy — an intentional and rewarding reflection of Rhoda Yee and her manuscript.

CONTENTS

PREFACE

This little cookbook primarily is a collection of favorite recipes previously shared only with my family, friends and students. Almost all of them are of Cantonese (Southern) origin and some are from my father's village where I grew up. Yet they aren't far out. All of the ingredients are readily available either in supermarkets or stores specializing in Chinese foods. And the tastes are delightful even to non-Chinese palates.

These recipes all have passed the tests of my severest critics: my parents, my family (especially my husband who also cooks), and all my students over the last six years. Many of them are make-aheads allowing you to entertain with ease.

But, most important, I feel the soul of Chinese cooking (or cooking from any country) is the culture of its people. To have some background and understanding of Chinese traditions and philosophy, hopefully, will give you added appreciation and enjoyment of the food. It is with this in mind that I share some of my experiences and recollections of life in my father's village.

I have many fond memories of different festivities and special occasions — the Chinese New Years' celebrations, a Chinese wedding, the baby's month-old party, to name a few. Then there are the every day happenings in the village, what we did for entertainment, how our days were spent and much more. Are you curious? Come, then. Let me be your guide on this very special tour.

THE WOKS, HOWS & WHYS

But first, we must detour.

As with all cookbooks, there is much preliminary information concerning basic equipment, methods and techniques that is both helpful and necessary. So let's pretend you are my student attending your very first class. At least you have one advantage. You don't have to take notes!

Equipment – Care and Usage

WOK:

Buying a wok is a wise investment since a good one will last a life time and will give you added pleasure when cooking Chinese food. Of ancient but scientific design, the wok is a bowl-shaped vessel used for stir frying, poaching, boiling, deep frying and steaming. Because of its high sides, the wok makes it easier to toss ingredients when stir frying without spilling. Less oil is needed because there is less area to be covered.

Many kinds of woks are available today. They are made of stainless steel, copper, aluminum, and both light and heavy weight rolled steel. Of all the materials, the heavy rolled steel type is by far the best since it will retain and sustain the high heat so essential in Chinese cooking.

A 14-inch wok is the best size for most kitchens since most burners (I'm talking about the large electric burners) won't provide sufficient heat to maintain the necessary high temperature of a larger wok. Besides, the 14-inch wok easily will accomodate a double recipe. Here's a good rule of thumb: it's easy to stir fry a little food in a large wok but never stir fry a lot of food in a small wok.

There is a popular misconception that a wok will not function satisfactorily on anything except a gas stove. Not true. A gas stove will give you the advantage of instant heat control but, aside from that, both gas and electric stoves give equal amounts of heat. It's just a matter of knowing how to use the electric range to your best advantage when stir frying.

To obtain the proper heat, set the wok on the large burner with the wide end of the ring stand facing up. This will allow the wok to sit closer to the electric coil, thus receiving maximum heat. (For a gas stove, invert the ring stand.)

Now, turn the heat to high (always use the highest heat available) and let the wok heat up for several minutes until it is hot. (It won't take as long on a gas range.) Add the oil and wait for it to heat before stir frying. Don't turn the heat down until you finish cooking! Follow this procedure and your wok will acquire sufficient heat.

A new wok must be treated or "seasoned" before using. During manufacture, a rust resisting coating is applied to the wok. This must be scrubbed off with heavy cleanser and scouring pads. Some coatings have a gummy, sticky finish. If this is the case, apply ordinary cigarette lighter fluid before scrubbing. This removes the sticky finish. After a good scrubbing, rinse thoroughly and fill with water. Cover and bring to a boil. Boil for 10 to 15 minutes. You'll see some brown spots appearing in

the wok. Don't panic. Just throw away the water and scrub it once more. After the last scrubbing and rinsing, place the wok over medium heat for 3 or 4 minutes or until all the moisture has evaporated. Rub a teaspoon of salad oil in the wok and work with a paper towel. Continue rubbing and adding a little oil until the towel comes out clean. Now the wok is ready to be used.

Each time you finish stir frying, place the wok in the sink, fill it with hot water and let it soak for 15 to 30 minutes. The soaking will loosen most of the food particles. Use a bamboo brush, sponge or soft cloth along with a very mild liquid soap to clean the wok. After rinsing and drying, set the wok over medium heat until all moisture has evaporated. Rub ¼ teaspoon salad oil into the wok to retain its glossy appearance.

This procedure must be strictly adhered to if you want to keep your wok in top condition. Although the wok will darken and mellow with age, there is no need ever to scrub or scour it. A Chinese cook never will trade an aged wok for a new one. Which reminds me of a little story:

A young Chinese bride who was brought up in Western cooking styles was invited to a family get together by her China-born mother-in-law. The young bride, eager to make a good impression, offered to help with the dishes. The mother-in-law was pleased with the thoughtfulness. But the pleasure turned to concern when, after a full hour, her daughter-in-law still was working in the kitchen. She investigated and nearly had a stroke as the young bride proudly displayed the wok she laboriously had scrubbed clean of all black traces!

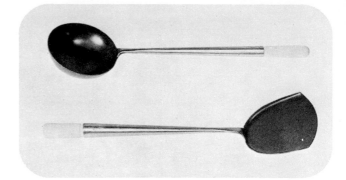

STIR FRY LADLE AND SPATULA:

These two are used together in stir frying. The spatula helps to turn the food while the ladle, poised at the tip of the spatula, helps to toss as well as contain the food within the wok. When the food is finished, it first is scooped up by the spatula and placed on the ladle. Then it is transferred to the serving platter. These two utensils are available in stainless steel or carbon steel. The latter requires the same care as the wok.

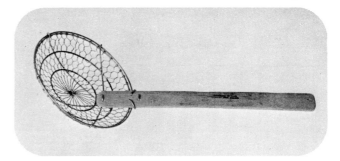

BAMBOO HANDLE WIRE STRAINERS:

These shallow strainers come in various sizes but a larger one probably will be more useful and practical. The bamboo keeps the handle cool for straining deep fried foods such as egg rolls and for boiling foods such as wontons and noodles.

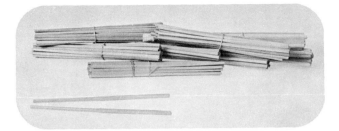

STEAMING:

A. Steaming Rack: This consists of two wooden sticks, each with a notch cut in the middle so the two fit to form a cross. It is placed over boiling water in the wok to serve as a platform for any heat-proof containers. A cover is placed over the wok to contain the steam.

B. Bamboo Steamer: This is a tiered steamer set over boiling water. The bottom of each tier is much like lattice work and allows live steam to circulate among the food placed on each layer. A lid over the top contains the steam. The food can be placed directly on the lattice work layers as when steaming pork buns. Or it first can be placed in a heat-proof dish and then set in the steamer as when making steam fish or steam pork. Since the steamers come in tiers, several different foods can be cooked at the same time thus saving time, fuel and space. Avoid storing steamers in dry, hot **places since the bamboo will buckle and break** around the seams. When not in use, they make unusual fruit bowls or they can become flower pots by placing a shallow dish with floral arrangements inside.

CHOPSTICKS:

The Chinese use chopsticks for cooking as well as eating. Although they come in various lengths, the longer ones generally are used for cooking and, because bamboo or wood can tolerate high heat, cooking chopsticks are made of either of these materials. In addition to cooking, they're used in every phase of food preparation such as beating eggs, stirring and mixing food, lifting out small pieces of food during cooking, turning and separating food in stir frying or deep frying, and testing the temperature of oil when deep frying. The latter is done by placing a clean and dry chopstick vertically in the middle of the hot oil touching the bottom of the wok. If many bubbles *immediately* rise along the side of the chopstick, the oil is ready for deep frying. As you can see, they double for beaters, forks, spoons, ladles, cooking thermometers, strainers and more.

To manipulate chopsticks, place one, about one quarter of its length from the top, between the thumb and the base of the index finger. The first knuckle of the fourth finger acts as a support. The second chopstick is held parallel above the first one resting between the crooked second and third fingers and pressing the tip of the thumb. You move only the second chopstick; the first remains stationary. It takes practice and patience. But once you master it, these two little sticks will become your best friends in the kitchen and at the dinner table.

CLEAVER:

The cleaver is a tool for cutting, dicing, mincing, slicing, chopping, mashing and scooping meats and vegetables. It comes in various weights. The lighter ones are used for slicing, mincing, etc., while the heavier ones are for heavy chopping or disjointing a chicken into bite size pieces. Because some chopping requires the blade to cut through bones, a heavier cleaver is more suitable. It will cut through bones with one clean, swift stroke eliminating bone splinters and messy looking pieces of meat.

Most cleavers are made of carbon steel but some stainless steel models are available. Carbon steel cleavers must be kept dry or they'll rust. They also should be oiled occasionally. When new, the carbon steel cleavers are coated with a rust resisting finish so they must be scrubbed thoroughly before using. Carbon steel cleavers are less expensive than stainless steel models but stainless steel cleavers don't rust and require only minimum care.

Since Chinese cooking is 10% cooking and 90% preparation (cutting, slicing, dicing, etc.), it's to your advantage to master the art of the cleaver. It'll save you hours of agony to say nothing of your irreplaceable fingers!

The cleaver appears to be a dangerous piece of equipment and probably will feel clumsy the first time you hold it but it's not difficult to get the knack. Two points must be considered: how you hold the food and how you hold and move the cleaver.

First, hold the food by placing your fingers vertically on top of the food. Arch your fingers a little so the finger tips are curved inward and tucked underneath. Your knuckles should be braced against the side of the cleaver.

Second, with the other hand, grasp the handle of the cleaver with the thumb and index finger gripping the upper part of the blade closest to the handle. Move the cleaver in a forward motion slanting the blade away from your fingers. Lift the cleaver no higher than ⅛-inch above the food you're cutting, pressing the side of the blade against your knuckles which act as a guard. Since your fingers are curved under, they'll always be safe from the sharp blade.

Now that you're adept with the cleaver, let's discuss the different types of cuts and their uses.

Straight Slicing: for cutting meats and vegetables. Always slice meat across the grain into ⅛-inch thicknesses.

Diagonal Slicing: For tougher, more fibrous vegetables such as celery and asparagus. Diagonal slicing exposes more inner surface and allows the vegetables to cook quickly.

Rolling Cut: For cylindrical or round vegetables such as carrots, cucumbers, turnips, potatoes and taros. Make a diagonal cut, then roll the vegetable one quarter turn and make the same cut again. Continue turning and cutting. This cut also allows maximum exposure of the inner surface and hastens the cooking time.

Cubing: Cut into 1-inch chunks.

Dicing: Cut into the size of a pea.

Mincing: Instead of putting it through a grinder, meat can be minced by chopping. You can

make it more fun if you use two cleavers (preferably the same weight) and, pretending you're a drummer, pound out a rhythm. It's not only fun, it's therapeutic. After you've chopped the meat in one direction, scoop it up and chop in the other direction.

Crushing: Flatten with the side of the blade as when crushing a chunk of fresh ginger or a clove of garlic.

Mashing or grinding: Mash several ingredients together in a bowl by using the cleaver handle. Do this when you're mashing salted black beans, fresh garlic and ginger to make a paste.

Basic Principles and Cooking Techniques

There are two basic steps in Chinese cookery: preparation and cooking.

First in the preparation phase is to dice, cut or slice the meats and vegetables to about the same size.

Second, always marinate your cut meats with corn starch, soy sauce, sugar, sherry and fresh ginger root. The marinade helps to tenderize and impart additional flavor to the meat.

Third, don't try to mix too many vegetables in any one dish or you'll end up with chop suey. Be selective. Use only one or two vegetables per dish as compliments to the meat.

For the cooking phase, you must master the stir fry technique. The first rule is that your wok must be extremely hot — as hot as you can stand it without burning the vegetables. The food must be cooked quickly so the meat juices are sealed in and the vegetables retain their colors, their vitamins and their crispness.

The second rule, add oil to the wok only after it is hot. Then allow the oil to heat before you start stir frying. Use peanut or vegetable oil, not butter or lard, since the latter two tend to burn easily. Don't be skimpy with the oil. Your food won't get oily if the pan is hot enough.

Third, stir fry each vegetable separately and set aside. This is because certain vegetables cook faster than others depending on their size, cut and water content. (You can stir fry two vegetables together provided they have approximately the same cooking time and your wok is large enough.)

Fourth, stir fry the meat only *after* you have stir fried all the vegetables. Pour in the sauce mixture when beef is almost done (for pork and chicken, pour sauce in when meat is finished.) As the sauce thickens the meat will get done at the same time. When doubling a recipe, it's better to stir fry the meat in two separate batches since too much meat cools down the wok and the meat becomes watery. Add stir fried vegetables after the sauce thickens, then quickly mix everything for a few seconds.

Fifth, Chinese food should be served hot (unless, of course, it's a cold dish). Like a souffle, it waits for no one.

Another popular cooking method is steaming. The food is cooked directly in a heat-proof serving dish set on a rack or in a bamboo steamer. The rack or steamer is placed over boiling water in a wok or pot. The boiling water produces the steam which cooks the food. Bring the water to a rolling boil after adding the dish. Then bring the heat down to medium — just enough to keep the steam going. Try not to lift the lid unless absolutely necessary. By absolutely necessary, I mean to check if the food is done or if more water is needed and for no other reason. If more water is necessary, add boiling water.

Your wok also is perfect for deep frying. In fact, it's far superior to a Western deep fryer. Because of its shape, you achieve the same depth as that of a deep fryer while using much less oil. Furthermore, greater space is available on top so more food can be fried at the same time.

Don't throw away used oil since it can be used once more for deep frying and thereafter for stir frying. Keep two bottles of used oil, separating the one used to fry seafood since it may have a slight fishy odor.

VISIT TO A CHINESE VILLAGE

Approximately 50 families, all with the same last name and all said to have been descended from one ancestor who started this community many hundreds of years ago, lived in our village. It was situated next to a river with the hills behind us and the rice paddies beyond them. Talk about ticky tacky little boxes — all of the houses were exactly alike in design and materials. Each had brick walls, concrete floors, red tile roofs and beautiful mahogany doors half a foot thick.

Each house was split level and symetrically designed. The first level was divided into three sections. The middle section was the living room with a 2-story high ceiling. The two side sections were divided into two rooms on each side with the front half of each used as the kitchen and the bedroom in the back.

Each kitchen had two stoves, one large and one small, made of bricks with a round hole on top in which the wok fitted perfectly. Fuels such as hay, kindling, wood or coal were fed through an opening in the front. We usually used hay for quick stir fry dishes. For cooking which took a longer time such as stewing or steaming, we'd switch to wood or coal.

Why in the world would you need two kitchens,

you ask? It always has been our custom to cook lots of food on all festive occasions, not only enough for the entire family (which could be several generations) but enough to pass out to the entire village. The women would start cooking days ahead and we kids used to snitch food to nibble all day. (That's another reason why we had to cook a lot.)

The front section of the living room had a moveable skylight, always open in good weather to allow sunlight and fresh air into the house. There were no other windows at the first level. Directly under our skylight was our atrium or, more appropriately, our gigantic Roman bath, kitchen sink and wash tub, all in one. It was about six feet by nine feet and six inches deep. Two big earthen tubs on each side contained water carried in from the river. We did all our washing here.

Against one living room wall was our 9-foot sofa made of magnificently carved mahogany. In fact, all of the living room furniture was mahogany, beautiful to look at but terribly uncomfortable unless you sat on cushions. Luckily, my mother and grandmother did lovely embroidery work, typical of many village women. Their handiwork not only cushioned living room sofa and chairs but was used as curtains in the doorways since there were no doors separating the rooms in the house.

Our flour mill was under the living room sofa. It consisted of two deep pits, one round and one square, made of polished stones inlaid at floor level about six feet apart. On the floor next to the square pit was a fulcrum with hinges attached to a thick, heavy beam spanning the length of the two holes. There also was a round mallet attached to one end which fit into the round hole.

Rice would be poured into the round pit while one or two people would stand next to the square pit at the other end, stepping down on the wooden beam with one leg. By stepping down, the beam would first be raised and then released allowing the mallet to strike the rice. Eventually, after several long, long hours, the rice would break down into fine particles while we'd collapse on the floor from exhaustion. Further sifting would produce home made rice flour.

As kids, we thought this was one of the most boring chores. Often, when we misbehaved, instead of getting a whipping, which we much preferred, we'd be marched straight to the flour mill where we did our one-legged flamingo dance while, supposedly, meditating on our naughty deeds. Needless to say, we always were on extra good behavior whenever my mother started to move the sofa! Or, more often, we'd disappear entirely!

The upstairs consisted of four bedrooms or storage areas, depending on the size of the family. During the rainy season, the river would rise and we'd frequently have floods. Then the whole family plus our portable stoves would move upstairs and we'd live there until the water receded.

Flood time always was fun time for the kids. We'd love to go down stairs to catch frogs, water snakes and fish. Since the water usually rose no higher than one or two feet, we could move fast enough to play blind man's bluff, tag or water polo. Looking back, I don't imagine the water was very clean but no one seemed to have gotten sick from playing in it or occasionally swallowing it. I guess we all had built up an immunity by then or else had cast iron stomachs.

LIFE IN THE VILLAGE

My aunt didn't have to work in the rice fields because, like most families in our village, she was able to hire another family from a different village to look after the fields. We also had a maid who did most of the domestic chores. I remember she was no more than 12 years old at the time and came from a very poor family. Since girls were considered excessive baggage in China, she was sold to my aunt when she was eight. She then became our housekeeper and kitchen helper but never the cook. Because all Chinese village women enjoy cooking, they'd never relinquish that pleasure to anyone else! The maid stayed with the family until she reached marriageable age at which time my aunt found her a suitable young man, she was married and regained her "freedom." This was a common and practical solution for many families who couldn't support their children. The girls were allowed to keep in touch with their own families and, in most cases, were treated fairly and well.

But, in spite of all the help, there still were many chores to be done. One of my most vivid memories concerned what seemed to be never-ending food preserving. Refrigeration was unheard of so we preserved by pickling, salting and sun drying. We did this with fish, beef, pork, duck and even vegetables.

There was a huge square at the entrance to our village where everyone hung clothes to dry. But, often, instead of clothes, you'd see strips of pork, whole fish, duck and strands of vegetables on the lines. Even the ground was covered with these foods and fruit.

During harvest, you'd also find huge trays of wheat and stacks of hay covering the square. Some of the funniest scenes I remember would occur whenever we had a sudden summer shower. The villagers would race out of their houses to the square trying to take down the drying food as quickly as they could. Every man, woman and child was mobilized. Dogs barked, pigs squealed, chickens squawked and everyone scrambled every which way.

A CHINESE BREAKFAST

I've often been asked what we ate for breakfast in China. When I was living in the village, we'd usually have rice with steamed salted fish or preserved sour vegetables — food with a strong taste to wake you up. Another favorite was "joak," a thick rice soup, with or without meat. Joak without meat usually was served with salted eggs on the side. The sharp contrasts in flavors would pop your eyes wide open. Pronto!

Joak (Thick Rice Soup)

Yield: Serves 4 to 8

1 cup long grain rice
5 quarts chicken stock
1 lb. ground pork
1 tbsp. dark soy sauce
1 tsp. salt
2 stalks green onions
12 water chestnuts

Condiments:

sesame oil

2-3 green onions, chopped fine

white pepper

½ cup tea melons (sweet cucumbers)
chopped fine

1 bunch Chinese parsley (cilentro) wash,
pat dry and cut into ½'' lengths

½ cup Szechwan turnips (or pickled
mustard)

½ cup chopped peanuts

Preparation: Rinse rice two or three times. Soak overnight. Mince green onions and water chestnuts. Mix with ground pork, soy sauce and salt.

Cooking: Bring stock and rice to a boil. Turn heat down and simmer for two to three hours or until the rice breaks down completely and the soup becomes thick and creamy. Turn heat up and add ground pork mixture, shaping one teaspoonful at a time into a small ball and dropping it into the soup. Cook for 5 minutes or until pork balls are done. Correct seasoning. Serve in individual soup bowls. Pass the condiments around for each person to choose his favorite toppings.

Do-ahead notes: Make ahead and reheat slowly.

Comments: Joak needn't be considered a breakfast-only dish. It's also good for lunch, dinner, or as a late evening snack.

Other kinds of meat such as ground beef, chicken slices or fish fillets can be substituted. A roast chicken or turkey carcass is excellent for making stock. Just cook the carcass, rice and water together. Take out the carcass when the soup is done.

Rice soup is satisfying, nutritious and easily digestible. It's an excellent food for those who are sick or have a stomach upset. To serve to the invalid, eliminate all meat to keep joak bland and fat free.

My favorite breakfast still is rice flour noodles mixed with soy sauce, oyster sauce, sesame oil, a dash of hot sauce and a generous sprinkling of toasted sesame seeds.

There was a peddler's stand right in front of our apartment house in Hong Kong (we moved to the city after I was older) and my mouth waters just thinking of the breakfast noodles he sold. For a quick and good substitute I use won ton skins and here's my recipe. You might prefer it for lunch rather than breakfast.

Breakfast Noodles (Gee Ma Wot Mein)

Yield: 1 serving

> ¼ **lb. won ton skins (about 20-25 sheets)**
> **2 tsp. oyster sauce**
> **1 tsp. light soy sauce**
> **½ tsp. sesame oil**
> **¼ to ½ tsp. hot sauce**
> **1 tsp. toasted sesame seeds**

Preparation: Cut won ton skins into ½-inch strips.

Cooking: Bring a small pot of water to a boil, drop won ton strips into the boiling water and boil for 1 minute. Rinse quickly with hot water and drain. Transfer to bowl and mix with the rest of the ingredients. Enjoy!

VISIT TO A TEA HOUSE

Lunch in our village was around 11 o'clock and usually consisted of rice, one or two steamed meat or fish dishes and one or two stir fried vegetables with or without meat.

Occasionally, in order to replenish our household supplies, we'd take a trip to the closest town, about a half day's walk. I always looked forward to the trip because it meant we'd get a chance to sample the many forms of pastries and dumplings found only in tea house lunches.

These delicacies, called "dim sum," are hors d'eouvres-like sweet and salty morsels served on tiny dishes. They're usually a minced meat filling wrapped in a rice flour dough and either are steamed or deep fried. In addition, there are meats, marinated and braised in a variety of delicious sauces.

Most working Chinese would go to the tea house for a small bite before starting work. The women would go there for brunch around eleven. Then, around noon, the working people would invade it again and pack themselves in like sardines. The whole place would vibrate with activity. Since Chinese don't eat sandwiches, there was no brown bagging. Besides, there were tea houses and roadside stands to fit everyone's budget, so that even rickshaw drivers and street peddlers could afford to eat out.

The following dim sum can be made ahead of time and frozen. They make terrific appetizers and take only about 10-15 minutes to reheat in the oven.

Egg Rolls (Chun Guen)

Yield: 24

1 package egg roll skins
2 cups cooked ham or barbecued pork
5 medium sized dried mushrooms
2 cups bamboo shoots
½ lb. fresh bean sprouts
3 stalks celery
2 stalks green onions
2 tbsp. oyster sauce
1 tsp. salt
1 tsp. sugar
4-5 cups oil for deep frying
1 egg, beaten

Preparation: Soak mushrooms for two hours, discard stems. Slice ham, mushrooms, bamboo shoots and onions to the size of a match stick. On the diagonal, slice celery into strips of the same size. Rinse bean sprouts in cold water. Drain well.

Filling: Heat wok, add 1 tbsp. oil. Stir fry separately and set aside: bean sprouts, 1 minute; celery, 2 minutes; mushrooms with bamboo shoots seasoned with sugar, 2 minutes; ham, 2 minutes, adding more oil as needed. Pour oyster sauce over ham and stir to mix. Return other ingredients plus the green onions and salt. Correct seasoning and cool.

Wrapping: Position wrapper like a diamond with the corners at top, bottom, left and right. Place about ⅓ cup of filling on lower section of wrapper. Tuck bottom corner around filling and roll *firmly* about half way up the sheet. Moisten the remaining three corners with beaten egg. Fold left and right corners toward the center and roll all the way up.

Frying: Heat oil in wok. Deep fry egg rolls on both sides until golden brown turning once. Drain on paper towels. Serve hot.

Do-ahead notes: Fry egg rolls. Cool. Just before serving, deep fry again.

Comments: Cut egg rolls into thirds with a sawing motion using a serrated knife. Don't press down or the filling will be squeezed out the other end. Fresh pork butt, prawns or chicken also may be used. If you're a vegetarian, you can do away with the meat entirely. Instead, add shredded Chinese cabbage, snow peas or onions.

Actually, we call these spring rolls rather than egg rolls. They're served during Chinese New Year to visiting friends and relatives and, since the New Year usually falls around February (the beginning of our spring), they came to be known as spring rolls. The name egg rolls came from dipping the wrapped rolls in an egg batter before deep frying. The traditional Chinese method is without the batter.

Curry Turnovers (Ga Lei Gok)

Yield: 48 appetizers or 10–12 luncheon size turnovers

½ lb. lean ground beef
12 water chestnuts, finely chopped
2 stalks green onions, finely chopped
2 tbsp. curry powder (more or less according to taste)
2 tsp. sugar
3 tbsp. catsup
½ tsp. salt
1 tsp. oil
3 tubes prepared, refrigerated crescent rolls*

Filling: Brown meat in 1 tsp. oil. Add all other ingredients except the rolls. Mix well and cool completely before wrapping.

Wrapping:

For appetizers: Unroll crescent rolls, separate dough from each tube into 4 rectangles and pinch the perforations between the two triangles together. Cut each rectangle into 8 squares. You should have 32 small squares all together. Place 1 tsp. filling on 16 of the squares. Top with the remaining squares. Pinch sides together and score with a fork.

For luncheon turnovers: Unroll dough and place two triangles together. Trim off the long side so that the three sides are equal in length. Pinch two of the three sides together and place 2-3 tbsps. of filling into the pocket. Pinch the third side shut. Score with fork.

Baking: Bake according to instructions on the tube.

Do-ahead notes: Wrap turnovers but do not bake. Freeze. When you wish to serve them, place frozen turnovers on greased cookie sheet in preheated oven and bake for 20-25 minutes at 375° until golden.

I have found the texture of these closest to the ones made from scratch.

Shrimp Toast (Ha Toe See)

Yield: 2 dozen

½ lb. fresh prawns
6 slices white sandwich bread
2 pieces 1-inch square fresh pork fat
8 water chestnuts
3 tbsp. cornstarch
1 tsp. salt
2 tbsp. sherry
1 small egg, lightly beaten

2 stalks green onions, chopped fine
Sesame seeds
Paprika

Preparation: Leave bread out on a platter for two hours to dry. Trim crusts and cut each slice into four squares. Shell, devein and clean prawns. Mince them into a fine pulp-like paste. Chop pork fat and water chestnuts until fine. Then mix with prawns, green onions, salt, sherry, cornstarch and beaten egg. Mix well and spread mixture on the bread, making a slight mound on each piece. Sprinkle sesame seeds and paprika on the filling and press lightly so they adhere to the mixture.

Cooking: Heat 4 cups of oil in the wok. Drop bread, shrimp side down, into oil and fry for 30 seconds. Turn and fry on the other side for another 30 seconds. (This is estimated time since it depends on how hot the oil is. Use your judgment.) Both sides should be golden. Drain on paper towel and serve hot.

Do-Ahead notes: Deep fry bread and mixture until it becomes a light beige, cool and freeze. To reheat, preheat oven at 350°, place frozen toast in a single layer on a cookie sheet and heat for 12 minutes. If toast already is thawed, reheat for 5 to 6 minutes. The toast will become a deeper brown as it's reheated.

Comments: To serve this as a luncheon dish, get a few extra prawns and slice each prawn in half lengthwise. Cut each piece of bread diagonally into two triangles and spread on mixture. Top with a halved prawn. Garnish as usual. Arrange toast on a round platter, pinwheel fashion. Top with a cherry tomato or parsley sprig in the center of the pinwheel.

16

Medallion Mushrooms (Gum Chin Doan Goo)

Yield: 24–30

24-30 medium sized fresh mushrooms
1 cup lean ground pork
4 medium sized prawns
6-8 water chestnuts, finely chopped
1 tbsp. dark soy sauce
1 tbsp. sherry
½ tsp. salt
½ tsp sugar
1 tsp. cornstarch
2 tsp. oil
½ cup chicken stock
4-5 tbsp. oyster sauce

Preparation: Wash and stem mushrooms. (Save stems for something else.) Pat dry. Shell and devein prawns. Mince them and mix with water chestnuts, pork, soy sauce, sherry, sugar, salt and cornstarch. Spread about 1 tsp. of filling onto each mushroom.

Cooking: Heat 2 tsp. oil in a skillet and place mushrooms in a single layer with the filling facing up. Brown for 1 minute. Pour ½ cup stock into the skillet, cover and simmer for 8-10 minutes, adding more stock if necessary. Uncover. (There should still be about ¼ cup stock left in the skillet.) Add oyster sauce and baste the mushrooms. When sauce thickens, mushrooms are ready to be served.

Do-ahead notes: This dish can be made ahead of time and reheated *slowly* on the stove, adding a little more broth and oyster sauce to make certain the sauce is not dried out.

Comments: Pick mushrooms that are about 1½ to 2 inches in diameter since they shrink during cooking. Insert toothpicks when serving as appetizers. These also can double as a dinner side dish.

Fried Won Ton with Sweet and Sour Sauce Dip

Yield: About 60–70

1 lb. won ton skins
½ lb. fresh ground pork
½ lb. fresh prawns
4 dried mushrooms, soaked for 2 hours
8 water chestnuts, finely chopped
2 stalks green onions, finely chopped
2 small eggs, beaten
¼ tsp. pepper
1½ tsp. salt

Preparation: Shell and devein prawns. Mince fine. Stem mushrooms and mince caps. Mix with prawns, pork, water chestnuts, green onions, half of the beaten eggs and all of the seasonings.

Wrapping: Place won ton squares on working surface so corners face up, down, left and right. Place 1 tsp. filling in the center of each skin. Dip a little of the beaten egg on the bottom corner, bring

top corner to meet bottom corner. Press to seal. Moisten left corner and bring right corner to meet it. Press to seal.

Frying: Heat 4 cups oil in wok. Fry wrapped won ton until golden. (About 2 min.) Turn over once. Drain. Serve hot.

Do-ahead notes: Deep fry won ton, cool·and freeze. To reheat, preheat oven at 350°. Place frozen won ton onto cookie sheet and heat for 12 - 15 min.

Sweet and Sour Sauce Dip

Yield: About 3 cups

> ½ **cup brown sugar**
> 1 **tsp. salt**
> ½ **cup vinegar**
> 1½ **tbsp. cornstarch**

4 **tsp. catsup**
¾ **cup pineapple juice**
1 **cup crushed pineapple**
A few drops red food coloring

Cooking: Mix cornstarch and pineapple juice in a sauce pan. Add remaining ingredients. Stir over medium-high heat until sauce thickens. Add more liquid if sauce needs thinning or more cornstarch if you want it thicker. You can use additional juice or vinegar depending on how sour you want the sauce.

Do-ahead notes: Make sauce, cool, place in glass jar, freeze. To reheat, thaw and reheat in small sauce pan.

Comments: You may substitute ground turkey for meat in won ton filling. However, since turkey is drier and more bland than pork, add a few more water chestnuts and ¼ tsp. monosodium glutamate to enhance flavor and texture.

Steamed Meat Dumplings (Siu Mai)

Yield: About 10 dozen

1 lb. ground pork sausage
1 lb. fresh ground pork
2 tsp. salt
15 water chestnuts, finely chopped
5 dried mushrooms
1 chunk ginger, the size of a quarter, crushed
½ cup cornstarch
½ cup water from boiled mushrooms

1 tbsp. light soy sauce
3 pieces salted turnips (each about 1-inch square), chopped fine
4 tbsp. sugar
1 tsp. teriyaki sauce
1 tsp. sherry
¾ tsp. sesame oil
½ cup Chinese parsley, finely chopped
1 pkg. won ton skins

Preparation: Place mushrooms, crushed ginger and 1 cup water in sauce pan. Bring to a boil and

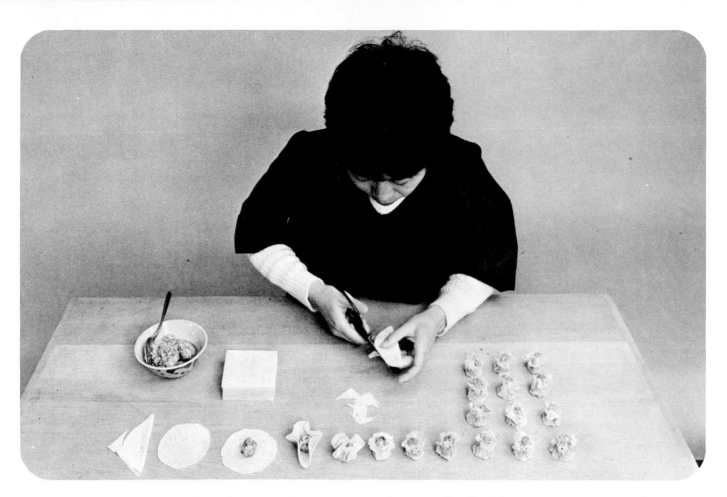

simmer for 15 minutes. Drain and reserve ½ cup liquid. Stem mushrooms and mince caps. Mix all ingredients except won ton skins.

Wrapping: Trim off 4 corners of won ton skins to form circles. Drop 1 tsp. mixture onto middle of the skins, gather up sides letting the skin pleat naturally. Flatten top and give the middle a light squeeze while tapping the bottom on a flat surface so it will stand upright.

Steaming: Arrange dumplings in an 8-inch round cake pan. Set pan on the steam rack in the wok. Fill bottom of wok with water. Cover. Steam for 15 minutes. Serve hot with a sesame oil and soy sauce dip (1 part sesame oil to 2 parts light soy sauce.)

Do-ahead notes: Steam dumplings, cool and freeze. Reheat by steaming again for 12-15 minutes.

Comments: Insert toothpicks for easy serving. If you use a bamboo steamer for steaming, place dumplings directly on the steamer without the cake pan. Steam for the same amount of time.

Parchment Chicken (Gee Bow Gai)

Yield: 16 wrapping packets

1 whole chicken breast
1 tsp. dark soy sauce
½ tsp. sherry

1 tbsp. minced green onion
1 tsp. minced fresh ginger root
½ tsp. sesame oil
5 dashes hot sauce
½ tsp. salt
1 tbsp. sugar

1 tsp. cornstarch
¼ tsp. garlic juice
1 tbsp. minced Chinese parsley
4 cups oil for deep frying
Cooking parchment

Preparation: Partially freeze chicken breast and slice it paper thin, across the grain, into thin strips. Marinate chicken in the rest of the ingredients for several hours or overnight. Cut cooking parchment into 4-inch squares.

Wrapping: Position parchment with corners at top, bottom, left and right. Drop about 1 tbsp. filling on lower corner of parchment. Tuck lower corner under filling and fold parchment about ⅓ way up. Fold left and right corners toward center, flatten filling and fold parchment paper once toward top corner. Tuck in top corner.

Cooking: Heat oil in wok. Drop wrapped chicken in oil and fry for 1½-2 minutes *at the most.* Drain on paper towel and serve hot.

Do-ahead notes: Deep fry, cool and freeze. To reheat, preheat oven at 350°. Heat frozen packets for 7-8 minutes.

Comments: Foil may be substituted if parchment paper is unavailable. If you prefer to serve fresh, wrap the filling several hours ahead and deep fry at the last minute.

MAH JONG, GHOST STORIES AND KICKING THE SWALLOW

Dinner was eaten early in the village, usually around four-thirty or five, and bedtime was around seven or a little later in summer. Often families would sit out in front of their houses and visit with neighbors. My grandmother was a marvelous story teller and we kids used to sit by the hour listening to some of her hair-raising ghost stories. Her stories were made even more scary when the night was dark, the only other sounds were crickets' songs and frogs' mating calls, and the only lights were faint glimmers from dancing fire flies.

The women liked to get together and cook, sew, quilt or embroider. But, best of all, they loved to play mah jong, a form of gin rummy using carved ivory tiles instead of cards. The men, too, enjoyed mah jong but they preferred fan tan, a game similar to dominos. They'd often get together at the one and only general store in the village for their bull sessions.

We kids didn't have any ready made toys to play with. They all were hand made. For instance, the girls would use two ends of burned incense sticks to make a cross. We'd pretend it was a doll and we'd cut out scraps from left over fabrics to make tops and trousers for our dolls.

Another popular home made toy was the swallow, made with three chicken wing feathers tied together. We'd stick the feathers through the centers of small stacks of tissue paper cut in 1-inch round circles. The bottom was weighted with a coin. The idea of the game was to kick the swallow with the inside of one's foot as many times as possible without having it land on the ground. Some kids were so accomplished they could keep it going 100 times or more! When we became more advanced, we'd try different kinds of kicks or switching kicks between the left and right feet.

Many of the games we played were similar to the ones kids play in this country. We'd often go into the hills to hunt "tigers" and pick wild berries or we'd go to the rice paddies and catch field mice and water snakes. Like kids everywhere, we were mischievous little devils.

THE DAILY FARES

Following are some of the everyday dishes we cooked when I lived in China. Of course, we used less meat. Also, we used unusual cuts of meat not readily available in today's markets. Therefore, I've made substitutions and included larger portions of meats while still keeping the authentic cooking methods and flavoring of the food.

This, then, is the beauty of Chinese cooking — the ability to adapt to changes to suit one's needs. You can easily substitute any kind of meat and vegetables in many of the recipes. The variations derived from one recipe alone are almost endless. What fun for us cooks!

SOUPS FOR ALL SEASONS

Most Chinese start dinner with soup. It's an integral part of any Chinese meal, as important as the salad dressing on the salad or the catsup on a hot dog. True, there are times when a cold plate of hors d'oeuvres is served in place of soup (you'll find this more often in Northern style cooking) but many Chinese will tell you a meal simply is not complete without soup. Some of my Caucasian friends can't understand why my husband and I have soup with our meals even in the middle of the hottest summer heat wave. Even though it's hotter than a firecracker outside, we drink our hot soup with beads of prespiration dripping down our foreheads. (And into our soup!)

Actually, it stems from habits formed in our childhoods. In China, refrigeration is rare, available only to the very wealthy city dwellers. All drinking water must be boiled for health reasons. Consequently, we always drank everything hot whether it was tea, soup or just plain water.

Good soup starts with a good broth. Always use either chicken or a combination of chicken and pork for the basic stock but rarely beef. Beef has a strong and hearty flavor, too dominating to blend compatibly with most of the meats and vegetables in our soups. Another reason is that beef was considered a luxury food item in China where steers were used as beasts of burden. Every inch of land was used for farming. Cattle-raising was unheard of. On the other hand, chickens and pigs were raised domestically and, since they impart a much lighter and delicate flavor, they blend in well with other soup ingredients.

Basic Chicken Stock

Yield: 2–2 ½ qts.

1 chicken
2 stalks green onions
1 tbsp. salt
**2-3 qts. water or just enough to
   cover chicken in pot**

Cooking: Bring all ingredients to a boil and simmer for 2 hours, skimming off skum and fat. Correct seasoning.

Comments: Store stock in ½ gallon milk cartons and freeze or freeze in ice cube trays. Swanson's chicken broth is a top notch substitute.

Basic Chicken and Pork Stock

Follow the above recipe but add 2 lb. pork bones and 1 lb. pork butt. Ham hocks also are excellent. Add more water since you have more ingredients.

SOUPS FOR A HOT SUMMER DAY

Here are four meatless soups which can be prepared in ½ hour or less. Such quick cooking retains much of the vitamins.

Watercress and Water Chestnut Soup (Sai Yeung Choy Tong)

Yield: 4–6 servings

2 bunches watercress
12 water chestnuts
1 qt. chicken stock

Preparation: Wash and rinse watercress several times until clean. Cut in half. Halve the water chestnuts.

Cooking: Bring all ingredients to boil and simmer, covered, for ½ hour.

Do-ahead note: Cook ahead and reheat before serving.

Chinese Cabbage Soup

(Ych Choy Tong)

Yield: 4–6 servings

1 small head Chinese cabbage
1 chunk ginger, the size of a quarter, crushed
1 tbsp. oil
1 qt. chicken stock

Preparation: Wash and cut cabbage into 1-inch lengths.

Cooking: Brown ginger in oil for 1 minute. Add cabbage and stock. Cover. Bring to a boil and simmer for 5-6 minutes.

Do-ahead notes: Brown ginger, add cabbage and stock but do not cook until 10 minutes before serving.

Fuzzy Melon Soup (Jit Gwa Tong)

Yield: 4–6 servings

2 6-inch long fuzzy melons (also called mo gua)
1 qt. chicken stock

Preparation: Remove skin from fuzzy melon with peeler. Wash and halve the melon lengthwise, then cut crosswise into ¼-inch slices.

Cooking: Combine melon slices with stock. Cover. Bring to boil and boil for about 5 minutes.

Comments: It's important that you don't overcook the sliced melon since it becomes mushy. When properly done, it's crunchy and has a very sweet taste, a sweetness that's natural and pure.

Peas and Egg Drop Soup

(Pea Dow Tong)

Yield: 4–6 servings

1 cup fresh or frozen green peas
1 2½-oz. can sliced mushrooms
2 eggs, beaten
1 qt. chicken stock

Cooking: Combine peas, mushrooms and stock. Bring to boil for 1 minute. Take off heat and add eggs, stirring until they separate in strands. Serve immediately.

SOUPS FOR A WINTRY NIGHT

Ah! When you take that very first sip, savor the rich and mellow flavor of each of these marvelously delicious soups. Your tired spirits will soar and your entire body will radiate warmth. It'll really hit the spot!

Winter Melon Soup
– Village Style (Doan Gwa Tong)

Yield: 8–10 servings

> **3 lb. winter melon**
> **6 dried oysters, soaked overnight**
> **6 dried red dates (or jujube nuts)**
> **1 slice tangerine peel, the size of a quarter, soaked overnight**
> **2 qts. pork and chicken stock**

Preparation: Use cleaver to cut off winter melon skin. (The skin is exceedingly tough.) Scoop out seeds and cut into 1-inch chunks. Wash and rinse oysters.

Cooking: Combine all ingredients and bring to a boil. Turn down heat and simmer for 3 hours.

Do-ahead note: Make ahead and reheat.

Turnip and Oxtail Soup (Lo Bak Tong)

Yield: 12 servings

> **2 medium sized Chinese turnips (lo-bak)**
> **1½-2 lb. oxtails (or beef shanks)**
> **1 large chunk ginger, the size of a silver dollar, crushed**
> **1 tbsp. oil**
> **1 star anise**
> **4 qts. chicken and pork stock**

Preparation: Peel turnips. Wash and, using rolling cut, cut into 2-inch chunks.

Cooking: In a large pot, brown crushed ginger in oil for 1 minute. Add oxtails and brown on all sides. Sprinkle salt on top. Add remaining ingredients. Bring soup to boil and simmer for 3-4 hours until oxtails are tender. Skim off fat before serving.

Do-ahead notes: Make the day before. The flavor improves the next day.

Comments: The Chinese turnip resembles a large horseradish. We use Japanese daikon as a substitute.

Sour and Hot Soup (Suen Lot Tong)

Yield: 6–8 servings

> **24 dried lily buds**
> **½ cup canned bamboo shoots**
> **1 can (1 lb. size) or 3 squares fresh bean cake (or dow fu)**
> **½ cup thinly sliced pork butt**
> **½ cup Szechwan turnips (ja-choy) or pickled mustard**
> **1 qt. chicken and pork stock**
> **1½ tsp. salt**
> **¼ tsp. ground white pepper**
> **2 tbsp. white vinegar**
> **1 tbsp. dark soy sauce**
> **2 tbsp. cornstarch mixed with 2 tbsp. water**
> **2 eggs, beaten**
> **2 tsp. sesame oil**

Preparation: Soak lily buds for 1 hour, drain and squeeze dry. Tie each bud into a knot and cut off the tough end. Cut bean cake, bamboo shoots and turnips into thin slices the size of match sticks.

Cooking: Bring stock, pork, lily buds, bamboo shoots and turnips to a boil. Add salt, white pepper, vinegar, soy sauce and bean cake and simmer for 2 minutes. Drizzle the cornstarch into the mixture and continue stirring until soup thickens. Remove from heat. Add beaten eggs, stirring until eggs separate into strands. Add sesame oil.

Do-ahead note: Make ahead and freeze.

Comments: My mother grew up in a household which included 75 people spanning four generations. My grandfather was a wealthy merchant (he had three concubines to prove his wealth) and his estate occupied several city blocks. The family employed two chefs, one Cantonese and one Northern, and although the wealthy consider cooking a menial task, my mother delighted in sneaking down to the kitchen to watch the chefs work. My grandmother would have skinned her alive if she knew my mother was learning to cook instead of doing embroidery, playing a musical instrument or just sitting around looking pretty. This sour and hot soup, as made by the Northern chef, is one of my mother's most treasured recipes.

Mongolian Fire Pot or Hot Pot

(Dah-Bin-Lo)

Yield: serves 4–6 people

> ½ **lb. flank steak**
> ½ **lb. chicken breast**
> ½ **lb. fillet of fish (any kind)**
> ½ **lb. prawns**
> 1 **small head Chinese cabbage**
> 1 **bunch spinach**
> 2 **squares bean cake (dow fu)**
> ¼ **lb. fresh mushrooms**
> ½ **lb. fresh egg noodles**
>
> **Meat and sea food marinade: (for each ½ lb.)**
> *2 tsp. sherry*
> *1 tsp. light soy sauce*
> *½ tsp. sesame oil*

Preparation: Slice flank steak, chicken breasts and fish fillets as thinly as possible. Shell, devein and clean prawns. Marinate each in separate bowls for 2 hours, then arrange them together on small individual plates, one plate for each person.

Par boil noodles for 3 minutes, rinse and drain. Place in bowl. Wash and clean vegetables, slice mushrooms thinly, cut bean cake into 1-inch by ½-inch by ¼-inch pieces. Slice Chinese cabbage into 2-inch by 1-inch pieces. Leave spinach leaves whole.

Prepare the following condiments and dips:
1. Sweet mixed ginger condiment: Slice contents of can of sweet mixed ginger into thin strips.
2. Soy-sesame oil dip: Mix 2 parts light soy sauce to 1 part sesame oil.
3. Oyster sauce dip: use bottled oyster sauce.
4. Hot mustard dip: Mix Chinese mustard powder with water until it becomes pasty. Add 2 or 3 drops vinegar if a hotter flavor is desired. Add a small amount of salad oil to give it a glossy appearance.
5. Plum sauce dip: Use canned plum sauce.
6. Hoisin sauce dip: 1 tsp. hoisin sauce, 1 tbsp. catsup, ¼ tsp. vinegar, ½ tsp. sugar and ½ tsp. dark soy sauce.
7. Sweet and sour sauce dip: Use the same one given for fried won ton.

Table setting: Place small individual meat and sea food plate on upper left of place setting. Set out dips and condiments in small soy sauce dishes directly above the setting. Center dinner plate. Place wire strainer on the left, chop sticks on the right. Place a soup bowl with Chinese soup spoon on upper right next to chop sticks.

Table top cooking: Place the hot pot, a round one is best, in the middle of the dining table. Heat broth to boiling. The diner places a small amount of meat in the wire strainer and dips it into the boiling broth for about 1 minute — just enough to cook through. Then he dips the cooked meat in the dip of his choice.

Toward the end of the meal, the hostess adds the noodles and vegetables to the broth. When they're cooked (about 3-4 minutes), the diner helps himself by ladling food into the soup bowl with his soup spoon.

Do-ahead notes: Do through preparation.

Comments: This is a marvelous meal-in-one-dish. It's a favorite among Chinese families particularly on a cold, wintry night. My children love doing the cooking themselves and it's amazing how much more eager they are to eat whenever we have hot pot for dinner! The broth has a most delicious flavor resulting from cooking the meat and sea food in it.

As for serving company, it's a wonderful, leisurely type of dinner with old friends or a great ice breaker for new acquaintances. If you have some one on your dinner list whose cooking *always* intimidates you, serve this and you'll be Numero Uno!

Other meats and vegetables you may use include lettuce, watercress, canned bamboo shoots, water chestnuts, canned abalone, oysters, lobster, shrimp, pork and ham.

WHAT IS A CHINESE CHICKEN?

During the years I lived in my father's village with my mother and grandmother, we had our own rice paddy, grew our own vegetables and raised chickens in the yard. The nearest store was in a small town about a half day's walk away. Three times a week, a man would go from door to door selling fresh beef or pork. Other than that, we provided all our own food.

When we were to have chicken for dinner, mother just picked one out from the yard and killed it. She dropped the chicken in a big pot of hot water for a short time, then we all helped pluck out the feathers and that was it.

When we were living in Hong Kong, my mother still raised chickens in our apartment. We had a dozen or so cooped up in individual cages in the room next to the kitchen. There was no place to let

them loose so they grew nice and plump from being caged up all day. We must have been the noisiest tenants in the building! Everytime we walked into the kitchen, all the hens would start clucking, thinking it was feeding time. And whenever one laid an egg, she'd cluck for hours letting the whole world know. When you have all twelve hens taking turns clucking, you can imagine the racket! When it came time to clean their cages — and I had the honor of being keeper of the pens — I wished I had not only ear plugs but nose plugs as well. Probably the only reason the landlord never objected was because he had a few chickens of his own.

Mother was especially proud of those fat hens. She was saving them for the Chinese New Year celebration, just a few weeks away. Chickens always were a must for any festive occasion and we all were looking forward to sinking our teeth into those plump, juicy hens.

But about a week before the celebration, two hoodlums broke into our apartment while we were there and took all our money, jewelry and other valuable possessions. Mother, fearful for our lives, was calm throughout the ordeal. But when the thieves started for the chickens — HER babies that she had raised since they were little chicks, OUR New Year feast — that did it! All her common sense left her and she yelled as loudly as she could, "Stop, you bums! Don't you dare touch a feather of my Chinese chickens!" That woke up all the hens and they began clamoring, thinking it was chow time. I don't know who made more noise but we woke up the entire building and the flustered thieves dropped everything and ran.

Even after we came to the United States, mother still preferred freshly dressed chickens, as do most Mainland Chinese. They believe the fresh dressed chicken has more of a chicken taste than frozen ones. In addition, the skin is much firmer and crisper, very important for making dishes such as white chop chicken. That's why there are so many poultry shops in Chinatown and, even though they cost more, mother always insists on buying Chinese chicken.

I agree there's a difference in taste and texture. But I'm not so particular and, being a practical person, I don't care to run to Chinatown everytime I make a chicken dish. I've had perfectly good results with fresh chickens from supermarkets. In fact, I only buy Chinese chicken when mother comes for dinner.

Chicken is, indeed, the most popular and versatile meat in the Chinese diet. It can be cooked whole by simmering, deep frying, steaming or roasting. It can be cut up for stir frying, steaming, braising or, again, deep frying. You can make stock with the giblets and bones or you can use the giblets for a most delicious rice stuffing. There is absolutely no waste. Every part of the chicken is used. In China, we even stir fry the innards — a tasty, crunchy dish. Believe me, our own brand of soul food goes back many centuries.

Here's a bit of general information on buying and cooking chickens. White meat should be cooked quickly because over-cooking causes it to become dry and stringy. It's usually saved for stir frying. Dark meat is juicier and smoother so it can stand a longer cooking time. We usually use it for steaming or braising. It's good practice to buy five or six fresh chickens at a time when they're on sale. Cut them up or bone them according to the types of dishes you plan to cook, then wrap them in the quantities needed for each meal. Label and freeze them. The chicken carcasses (consisting of the backs, breast bones, necks and giblets) go in a big soup pot to become chicken stock. This also can be frozen.

White Chop Chicken (Bak Juhm Gai)

Yield: 4 servings

1 3-lb. fryer
1 tsp. salt
1 green onion
Water
¼ cup salad oil

Preparation: Wash and rinse chicken under warm water to bring to room temperature. In a small sauce pan, heat oil and then let it cool.

Cooking: Place chicken in a pot into which it just fits. Add enough water to cover chicken. Take chicken out. Add salt and green onion and bring to a boil. Lower chicken into pot and bring water back to a boil. Cover pot, turn off heat and let chicken steep for 1 hour. Lift chicken out, rinse under cold water, drain and pat dry. Brush skin with the cooled salad oil. Generously sprinkle additional salt over entire chicken. When cool, chop chicken into 1-inch by 2-inch pieces. Arrange attractively on a platter and serve with one or both of the following dips:

Green onion dip:
    ¼ cup oil
    3 tsp. salt
    2 stalks green onions

  Heat, then cool oil mixed with salt. Shred green onions lengthwise and cut into 1-inch lengths. Place the oil and salt mixture in one dish and green onions in another. The diner picks up a small piece of green onion along with the chicken and dips both into the salt-oil mixture.

Oyster sauce dip: Simply pour bottled oyster sauce into a small dish.

Do-ahead notes: Cook and chop chicken an hour ahead. Cover. It should be served at room temperature.

Comments: This is one recipe where a freshly dressed chicken will make a great difference in taste and texture. NEVER cook the chicken until the meat falls off the bone. That is why it is much better to steep rather than to simmer the chicken since you are less likely to over-cook it. The cold water rinse helps stop the chicken from further cooking and also helps "crisp" the skin.

Plum Sauce Chicken (Muy Jeung Gai)

Yield: 4 servings

1 white chop chicken
¾ cup plum sauce
2 tbsp. sugar
1 tbsp. vinegar
¼ cup pineapple juice
½ cup pineapple chunks
8-12 maraschino cherries
½ cup sweet mixed gingers
2-3 tbsp. toasted sesame seeds

Preparation: Mix plum sauce, sugar, vinegar and pineapple juice. Let stand 1 hour or over night in the refrigerator.

Assembling: Chop and arrange chicken on serving platter. Decorate with pineapple chunks, cherries and sweet mixed gingers. Pour plum sauce mixture over chicken and sprinkle with toasted sesame seeds. Serve.

Do-ahead notes: Pour half of the plum sauce mixture over chicken. Cover and return to refrigerator. Just before serving, pour the rest of the plum sauce mixture over chicken and garnish with toasted sesame seeds.

Comments: This is a chicken dish that is both delicious and beautiful to behold. It's an ideal entree for a hot day. Fried rice is an excellent accompaniment.

Sesame Chicken (Gee Ma Gai)

Yield: 4 servings

>   1 white chop chicken
>   2 tbsp. light soy sauce
>   2 tbsp. teriyaki sauce
>   1 tsp. sesame oil
>   1 tsp. salad oil
>   1 tbsp. fresh ginger, minced
>   2 tsp. sugar
>   2-3 tbsp. toasted sesame seeds
>   A few sprigs of Chinese parsley

Preparation: Mix all above seasonings except sesame seeds and parsley.

Assembling: Chop and arrange chicken on platter. Pour sauce over and garnish with toasted sesame seeds and Chinese parsley.

Do-ahead notes: Cook and chop chicken an hour ahead. Cover. Pour sauce over chicken and garnish just before serving. It should be served at room temperature.

Soy Sauce Chicken (See Yao Gai)

Yield: 4 servings

>   1 3-lb. fryer
>   2 cups dark soy sauce
>   1 cup water
>   8 tbsp. sugar
>   1 star anise

>   1 chunk fresh ginger root, the size of a quarter, crushed
>   1 stalk green onion, shredded lengthwise and cut in 1-inch lengths

Preparation: Wash and pat chicken dry. Mix soy sauce, water, sugar, star anise and ginger in a pot which just fits the chicken.

Cooking: Bring soy sauce mixture to a boil. Lower chicken into pot and bring back to a boil. Cover. Simmer for 12 minutes. Turn chicken over and simmer for another 12 minutes. Lift chicken out and cool on platter for ½ hour. Chop chicken into 1-inch by 2-inch pieces and arrange on platter. Pour ¼ cup of the sauce over chicken. Garnish with shredded green onion.

Do-ahead notes: Cook chicken an hour ahead. Cool and chop. Cover. Garnish and pour sauce over chicken just before serving. If the sauce has cooled, warm it up.

Comments: The sauce will keep for months in the refrigerator if you boil it occasionally. It can be used for the above recipe three or four times. You also can use the sauce for marinating steaks, chops or chicken for barbecue.

Soy Sauce Chicken Wings

(See Yao Gai Yik)

Use about 16 chicken wings. Cut wing tips off and save for making stock. Prepare as in soy sauce chicken except simmer only 10 minutes. Then let wings soak in the sauce for 45 minutes. Turn chicken wings several times during soaking period to insure even coloring.

Steamed Chicken with Mushrooms and Lily Buds (Dong Goo Jing Gai)

Yield: 2–3 servings

1 3-lb. fryer, using only dark meat
4 dried mushrooms
18 dried lily buds
3 pieces fresh ginger, the size of a quarter
1 tbsp. cornstarch
2 tsp. salt
1 tbsp. dark soy sauce
1 tsp. sugar
1 tsp. sherry

Preparation: Chop dark meat, bones and all, into ¾-inch pieces. Soak mushrooms and lily buds until soft. Stem mushrooms. Thinly slice mushroom caps and fresh ginger. Tie a knot in each lily bud and cut off tough ends. Mix all ingredients and pat into a heat–proof dish.

Cooking: Place heat–proof dish on steaming rack in wok. Fill bottom of wok with water and cover. Bring water to a boil, turn heat to low and simmer for ½ hour.

Do-ahead notes: Do through preparation. Steam just before serving.

Comments: The chicken can be kept warm in the steamer for several hours and still retain the same taste and texture. It is better to use a wide shallow dish for steaming rather than a deep one because, aside from achieving a better appearance, the food cooks faster.

Coriander Chicken Salad (Sow See Guy)

Yield: 10–12 servings

2 lb. chicken parts
Chicken marinade:
2 tbsp. light soy sauce
1 tbsp. sherry
1 tsp. sugar
Dashes of garlic powder, salt and pepper
2 tsp. fresh ginger, minced
1 2-oz. pkg. bean thread (also known as long rice)
2 stalks green onions
1 medium head iceberg lettuce
1 bunch coriander (also known as cilentro or Chinese parsley)
½ tsp. dry mustard
½ tsp. each salt and pepper
1 tbsp. salad oil
2 tbsp. sesame oil
2 tbsp. light soy sauce
1-2 tbsp. vinegar
3 tbsp. toasted sesame seeds

Preparation: Place chicken in marinade for several hours. Bake, skin side up, in 350° oven for 45 minutes. Cool and shred chicken by hand into small pieces. Heat oil, drop small batches of bean thread into oil. The bean threads will puff up immediately. Take out and drain. Shred green onions and lettuce. Wash and cut coriander into 1-inch lengths.

Assembling: Place chicken, lettuce, green onions and coriander in large salad bowl or pot and mix with dry mustard, salt and pepper. Toss to mix well. Add sesame oil, salad oil, soy sauce, vinegar, toasted sesame seeds and ¾ of the fried bean thread. Mix again. Transfer salad to a large serving tray and top with remaining bean thread.

Do-ahead notes: Bake and shred chicken and fry bean thread the day before. Store bean thread in an air tight container. Shred the greens early in the day and keep in plastic bags. Toss salad just before serving.

Comments: You must use fresh oil to fry the bean thread so the noodles puff up better. The oil must be very hot. Otherwise, the noodles will be only partially puffed and will have hard interiors. You may substitute fresh watercress if coriander is unavailable.

Chicken Medallions with Snow Peas

(Gai Bang Chow Suet Dow)

Yield: 4 servings

Chicken medallion mixture:
1 whole chicken breast
12 water chestnuts
1 stalk green onion
1 tbsp. cornstarch
1 tsp. light soy sauce
A few dashes garlic powder
½ tsp. sherry
1 tsp. sugar
½ tsp. salt

½ lb. snow peas
1 red bell pepper
4 tbsp. oil

Sauce mixture:
1 ½ tsp. cornstarch
1 tsp. sugar
½ cup chicken stock
½ tsp. vinegar
½ tsp. sesame oil
1 tsp. light soy sauce
¼ tsp. salt

Preparation: Mince chicken breast, water chestnuts and green onions. Combine with the rest of the medallion mixture. Shape into small balls and flatten between sheets of oiled waxed paper. Wash and string the snow peas. Cut bell peppers into ½-inch chunks. Mix sauce mixture.

Cooking: Heat wok. Pour in 1 tbsp. oil and heat. Stir fry snow peas for 1½ minutes. Season with dashes of salt and sugar and set aside. Add 1 tbsp. oil to wok and stir fry red bell pepper for 1 minute.

Set aside. Pour 2 tbsp. oil into wok and reheat. Add chicken patties, a few at a time, lower heat to medium and brown evenly on both sides. Stir the prepared sauce mixture and pour over the chicken medallions. Stir until sauce thickens. Add vegetables and mix well.

Do-ahead notes: Do through preparation.

Chicken Cashew

Yield: 4 servings

2 cups chicken breast, cut in ½-inch slices

Marinade for chicken:
1 tbsp. light soy sauce
1 tbsp. sherry
1 tbsp. cornstarch
½ tsp. each sugar and salt

1 cup peas, fresh or frozen
¾ cup celery, diced
¾ cup onions, diced
¾ cup red bell pepper, diced
½ to 1 cup cashew nuts
1 2½-oz. can whole button mushrooms
   (reserve liquid)

Sauce mixture:
   ½ cup reserved mushroom liquid
   2 tsp. cornstarch
   1 tsp. light soy sauce

1 clove garlic, crushed
1 chunk ginger, the size of a
   quarter, crushed
4 tbsp. oil

Preparation: Mix sliced chicken with marinade and let stand for 15 minutes. Prepare sauce mixture.

Cooking: Heat wok, pour in 1 tbsp. oil and heat. Stir fry celery and onions for 1-2 minutes. Season lightly with salt and sugar. Set aside. Add 1 tbsp. oil and stir fry peas with red bell peppers for 1-2 minutes, also season lightly with salt and sugar. Set aside. Add 2 tbsp. oil and stir fry chicken until done. Stir the prepared sauce mixture and pour over chicken, stirring until sauce thickens. Add vegetables, then add cashew nuts. Mix well and serve.

Do-ahead notes: Do through preparation.

Comments: Here's a little secret. What do you get when you omit the onions, peas, celery and cashews and substitute water chestnuts, bamboo shoots and walnut halves? Da-Dum! One Chicken Walnut coming up! And if you leave the original recipe intact but substitute whole almonds for cashews? Voila! Chicken Almond Ding!

Five Spice Game Hens

(Siu Yeah Gai)

Yield: 4 servings

   4 Cornish game hens
   1 tbsp. five spice powder
   2 tbsp. salt
   1 tbsp. plum sauce
   2 tbsp. bean sauce
   2 tbsp. hoisin sauce
   1 tbsp. sherry
   ¼ cup dark soy sauce
   ¼ cup maple syrup

Preparation: Wash and clean game hens. Pat dry and rub cavities with five spice powder. Mix hoisin sauce, bean sauce, sherry and plum sauce. Rub cavities with half the sauce. Rub skins with the remaining sauce mixture plus salt. Let stand overnight. Mix soy sauce and syrup.

Cooking: Preheat oven at 350°. Rub skins of game hens with soy sauce and syrup mixture. Roast back side up for 20-25 minutes. Turn breast side up and roast for another 20-25 minutes until the skins turn golden brown.

Do-ahead notes: Do through preparation.

Comments: Use the same recipe for roast chicken. Seven flavor rice or fried rice are good accompaniments.

Pork – A Meat for All Purposes

Pork is preferred over beef in Chinese cooking. Pork has a more delicate flavor and is much more versatile. It's used in making stock, in stir frying with vegetables, in steaming with other Chinese dried or canned goods, in deep frying as in sweet and sour pork and in barbecuing.

Buy one or two 4-5 lb. boneless pork butts and slice them into ¾-1 lb. pieces. Wrap and label each piece before freezing. This way, you take out only what you need each time. Buy ground pork for dishes requiring minced pork. If none is available, get a pork butt and ask the butcher to grind it. Divide into ½-1 lb. portions, wrap, label and freeze.

Barbecued Pork (Char Siu)

Yield: 6–8 servings

> 1 3-3½-lb. boneless pork butt
> 2 tbsp. hoisin sauce
> 4 tbsp. catsup
> 4 tbsp. sugar
> 1 tbsp. dark soy sauce

Preparation: Cut pork butt into 4-inch by 2-inch by 1-inch strips. Mix rest of ingredients and pour over pork pieces. Marinate at least 4 hours or overnight.

Cooking: Preheat oven at 375°. Line roasting pan with foil and place pork on roasting rack. Roast a total of 45 minutes, turning over once or twice.

Do-ahead notes: Barbecued pork can be made anywhere from a few days to two weeks in advance. Just wrap and freeze. For cold appetizers, thaw, then slice just before serving. To reheat, thaw first and reheat in a slow oven until just heated through (about 20 minutes). Delicious either way.

Comments: This is the most basic and versatile pork recipe. We use it in fried rice, egg rolls, stir fry with vegetables, and in egg dishes such as egg foo young. You may serve it as a hot or cold appetizer or use it as a garnish on top of noodles.

Barbecued Spareribs (Siu Pie Quat)

Buy about 3 lbs. spareribs. Marinate as in above recipe. Hang ribs by using metal shower curtain hooks hanging from the top oven rack. Place a shallow pan of water on the bottom oven rack to catch drippings. Roast according to preceeding recipe.

Steamed Spareribs in Black Bean Sauce (Dow See Jing Pie Quat)

Yield: 4 servings

> 1 lb. spareribs
> 1 clove garlic, minced fine
> 2 tbsp. salted black beans
> 1 tbsp. fresh ginger, minced
> 1 tsp. dark soy sauce
> 1 tbsp. cornstarch
> 1 tbsp. sherry

Preparation: Have butcher cut spareribs into 1-inch pieces. Trim off fat. Place spareribs in a heat proof dish. Wash and rinse black beans 2 or 3 times, then mash them with garlic, ginger, soy sauce, cornstarch and sherry. Mix with spareribs.

Cooking: Place heat proof dish on steaming rack in wok. Add water to bottom of wok. Cover. Steam for 30 minutes.

Do-ahead notes: Do through preparation.

Comments: Spareribs can be left in the steamer for 2 hours if dinner is late. Substitute bean sauce for salted black beans — and abracadabra! Mein See Jing Pie Quat! (Steamed Spareribs in Bean Sauce.)

Steamed Minced Pork with Water Chestnuts (Ma Tai Jing Gee Yuke)

Yield: 4 servings

> **1 lb. ground pork**
> **12 water chestnuts, minced**
> **2 tsp. salt**
> **2 tbsp. dark soy sauce**
> **½ tsp. sugar**
> **1 tbsp. cornstarch**

Preparation: Mix all ingredients well and pat out evenly in a heat proof dish.

Cooking: Place dish on steaming rack in wok. Fill bottom of wok with water. Cover. Steam for 30 minutes.

Do-ahead notes: Do through preparation.

Comments: If you like your food hot and spicy, add ½ cup chopped Szechwan turnips (ja-choy), reduce salt to ½ tsp. and add 1 more tsp. sugar. You'll have a new dish, Steamed Pork with Szechwan Turnips (Ja Choy Jing Gee Yuke).

Dow Fu and Pork in Bean Sauce

(Dow Fu Yuke)

Yield: 4 servings

> **1 large cake of dow fu (bean cake) or 4 small ones**
> **½ lb. lean pork butt**
> **1 tbsp. cornstarch**
> **2 tbsp. dark soy sauce**
> **3 tbsp. bean sauce**
> **1 tbsp. sugar**
> **¼ cup water**
> **1 stalk green onion, chopped fine**
>
> **Sauce mixture:**
> *1 tsp. cornstarch*
> *¼ cup water*
> *2 tbsp. oyster sauce*
>
> **2 tbsp. oil**

Preparation: Slice pork butt into ⅛-inch pieces. Marinate with cornstarch and soy sauce for ½ hour. Cut dow fu into ½-inch cubes. Prepare sauce mixture.

Cooking: Heat wok. Add 2 tbsp. oil and heat. Stir fry pork until almost done, about 1½-minutes at most. Add bean sauce, sugar, water and dow fu. Mix lightly, careful not to break up the dow fu. Cover and cook over low heat for about 3-5 minutes or until dow fu is just heated through. Add the sauce mixture and stir until thickened. Sprinkle with green onions and serve.

Do-ahead notes: Cook ahead and reheat slowly on low heat.

Comments: Dow fu in bean sauce is a favorite combination, like sour cream in beef stroganoff. Since dow fu is bland, it readily takes on the flavor

Sweet and Sour Pork (Goo Lo Yuke)

Yield: 6 servings

1 lb. pork butt cut into 1-inch chunks

Meat marinade:
1 tbsp. sherry
1 tbsp. water
2 tbsp. Kikkoman soy sauce (this brand is best for this recipe)
4 tsp. flour
4 tsp. cornstarch

1 green pepper, cut into ½-inch chunks
1 onion, cut into wedges
12 maraschino cherries
1 cup canned lichee
1 cup pineapple chunks

Sauce mixture:
½ cup brown sugar
½ cup vinegar
1 tsp. salt
4 tbsp. catsup
¾ cup pineapple juice
4 tsp. cornstarch

Preparation: Drain fruits, prepare sauce mixture. Marinate pork in meat marinade for ½ hour.

Cooking: Deep fry pork cubes in wok for about 3-4 minutes until golden brown. Drain. Pour all the oil back into the bottle. Add sauce mixture into wok and stir until thickened. Add green pepper and onions and cook for 2 minutes. Add pork cubes and stir until heated through. Add fruits and stir until they're coated with the sauce.

Do-ahead notes: Cook through making the sauce. Just before serving, add pork, vegetables and fruit according to directions.

of the bean sauce. By adding a little oyster sauce, it becomes a very rich and smooth-tasting dish.

Steamed Chinese Pork Sausages

(Jing Lop Cheong)

Yield: 2 servings as a side dish

1 pair Chinese sausages (lop cheung)

Preparation: Cut sausage diagonally into ¼-inch slices. Place in a heat proof dish.

Cooking: Place dish on steaming rack in wok. Fill bottom of wok with water. Cover. Steam for 15 minutes. Drizzle 1 tbsp. light soy sauce over sausages.

Do-ahead notes: Do through preparation.

Comments: The sausages can be steamed right on top of the rice. Simply place sliced sausages on top of the rice when it comes to a boil. Continue cooking rice as directed in the boiled rice recipe. When rice is done, take out sausages and serve.

Variations on a Flank Steak

Whenever we use beef for stir fry dishes, flank steak is the most popular cut. Since there are only two flank steak cuts from each steer, many meat markets have a tendency to run short. Therefore, it's a good idea to buy several so you'll have some on hand when you need them. Cut flank steaks along the grain into large portions — enough to suit the needs of your family — then label and freeze them. If you can't find flank steaks, substitute sirloin, round or chuck steaks.

Ginger Beef (Gueng Choan Gnow Yuke)

Yield: 4 servings

1 lb. flank steak
Meat marinade:
 1 tbsp. cornstarch
 1 tsp. sugar
 2 tbsp. light soy sauce
 3 tbsp. fresh ginger, minced
 1 tsp. sherry

5-6 medium dried mushrooms, soaked for 2 hours
1 8½-oz. can bamboo shoots
1 chunk ginger, the size of a quarter, crushed
2 cloves garlic, crushed
¼ tsp. salt
½ tsp. sugar
1 tbsp. chicken stock
2 stalks green onions
3 tbsp. oil

Sauce mixture:
 2 tsp. cornstarch
 ½ cup chicken stock
 2 tbsp. oyster sauce

Preparation: Cut flank steaks into ⅛-inch thick slices across the grain and marinate for 15 minutes. Stem mushrooms and slice caps ¼-inch thick. Cut the whole bamboo shoots lengthwise in half, then slice cross-wise into ⅛-inch thick pieces. Cut green onions into 1-inch lengths. Prepare sauce mixture.

Cooking: Heat wok. Pour in 1 tbsp. oil and heat. Stir fry bamboo shoots with sliced mushrooms. Add ¼ tsp. salt, ½ tsp. sugar and 1 tbsp. chicken stock. Stir fry 1 minute. Set aside. Pour 2 tbsp. oil into wok. Brown the crushed ginger and garlic for 1 minute. Set aside. Add beef. Stir fry until almost done. Add sauce mixture and stir until thickened.

Add mushrooms, bamboo shoots and green onions. Mix well and serve.

Do-ahead notes: Cook up through stir frying the mushrooms and bamboo shoots. Do the rest of the cooking just before serving.

Oyster Sauce Beef (Ho Yow Gnow Yuke)

Yield: 4 servings

1 lb. flank steak
Meat marinade:
 1 tbsp. cornstarch
 1 tsp. sugar
 ½ tsp. salt
 ½ tsp. sherry
 2 tbsp. light soy sauce
1 medium onion, cut into wedges
1 medium green pepper, cut into 1-inch chunks
¼ tsp. salt
1 tbsp. chicken stock
2 cloves garlic, crushed
4 tbsp. oyster sauce
3 tbsp. oil

Preparation: Cut flank steak across the grain into ⅛-inch thick slices. Mix with meat marinade for 15 minutes.

Cooking: Heat wok. Pour in 1 tbsp. oil and heat. Stir fry onion and green pepper together for 1 minute. Add salt and stock and stir fry until liquid has evaporated. Set aside. Pour 2 tbsp. oil into wok and brown garlic for 45 seconds. Discard garlic and add beef. Stir fry until ¾ done, about 1 minute, and add oyster sauce. Mix well. Add vegetables, stir for a few seconds and serve.

Do-ahead notes: Do through preparation.

Tomato Beef Curry

(Ga Lei Fon Kare Gnow Yuke)

Yield: 4 servings

1 lb. flank steak
Meat marinade:
  1 tbsp. cornstarch
  1 tbsp. light soy sauce
  1 tbsp. sherry
1 medium onion, cut into 1-inch chunks
2 medium tomatoes, cut in wedges
1 medium green pepper, cut in wedges
1 tbsp. brown sugar
1 tsp. salt
2 tbsp. curry powder
4 tbsp. catsup
1 tbsp. oyster sauce
3 tbsp. oil

Preparation: Slice flank steak ⅛-inch thick across the grain. Marinate for 15 minutes. Sprinkle brown sugar over tomato wedges.

Cooking: Heat wok. Add 1 tbsp. oil and heat. Stir fry onion with green pepper for ½ minute. Add 1 tbsp. water, cover for ½ minute, uncover and stir until water has evaporated. Set aside. Pour 2 tbsp. oil into wok and stir in the curry powder. Let the flavor release (a few seconds) and add beef and salt. Stir fry until ¾ done, about 1 minute. Add tomato wedges. Stir until just heated through. Add catsup and heat until sauce bubbles. Add all other vegetables and oyster sauce. Mix well.

Do-ahead notes: Do through preparation.

Skewer Beef (Siu Gnow Yuke)

Yield: 4 servings

1 lb. flank steak
Meat marinade:
  3 tbsp. light soy sauce
  3 tbsp. dark soy sauce
  2 tbsp. sugar
  4 tbsp. sherry
  2 cloves garlic, minced
  4 tbsp. fresh ginger, minced
  4 tbsp. sesame oil

Preparation: Unroll the entire flank steak. Trim off fat. Cut into ⅛-inch slices across the grain. Marinate at least 4 hours. String sliced beef on bamboo skewers like ribbon candy.

Cooking: Barbecue over charcoal or set oven to broil. Brown 4 inches away from broiler for just a few minutes, turning over once to brown both sides.

Do-ahead notes: Do through preparation.

Beef Asparagus

(Lei Suen Chow Gnow Yuke)

Yield: 4 servings

1 lb. flank steak
Meat marinade:
  1 tbsp. cornstarch
  1 tbsp. light soy sauce
  1 tsp. sherry
  ¼ tsp. sugar
  ¼ tsp. salt

1-1½ lb. asparagus
¼ tsp. salt
1-2 tsp. chicken stock
2 tbsp. black beans
1 clove garlic, minced
2 tbsp. fresh ginger, minced
1 tsp. dark soy sauce
1 tsp. water
3 tbsp. oil

Sauce mixture:
  2 tbsp. cornstarch
  ½ cup chicken stock

Preparation: Cut flank steak into ⅛-inch thick slices across the grain. Marinate for 15 minutes. Break off tough ends of asparagus and discard. Wash and cut asparagus diagonally into ½-inch thick slices. Wash black beans and mash with garlic, ginger, soy sauce and water. Prepare sauce mixture.

Cooking: Heat wok. Add 1 tbsp. oil and heat. Stir fry asparagus with ¼ tsp. salt for 1 minute. Add 1 tsp. stock, cover and cook over high heat for 1-2 minutes until asparagus is tender yet crunchy. Add more stock if necessary. Set aside. Add 2 tbsp. oil and stir fry meat with black bean mixture for 1 minute. Add sauce mixture. Stir until thickened. Add asparagus and mix well. Serve.

Do-ahead note: Do through preparation.

Steak Balls (See Dick Kow)

Yield: Serves 4

1½ lb. top sirloin
Meat marinade:
  1 ½ tbsp. cornstarch
  2 tbsp. light soy sauce
  1 tsp. sugar
  1 tbsp. sherry
1 green pepper, cut into chunks
1 medium size onion, cut into wedges
½ lb. small size fresh mushrooms
Sauce mixture:
  1 tbsp. hoisin sauce
  1 tbsp. bean sauce
  ¼ cup chicken stock
  1 tsp. cornstarch
  3 tbsp. oyster sauce
5 tbsp. oil

Preparation: Cut meat into 1-inch cubes. Add marinade and let stand for 4 hours. Wash and drain fresh mushrooms, leave whole. Prepare sauce mixture.

Cooking: Heat wok until hot. Add 1 tbsp. oil and stir fry pepper with onion for 1 minute. Set aside. Add 1 tbsp. oil and stir fry mushrooms for 1 minute, add 1 tbsp. sherry as you stir fry. Set aside.

Divide meat cubes into three batches and stir fry each batch separately with 1 tbsp. oil each time until brown on all sides. Set aside. Pour in the sauce mixture and stir until bubbly. Add back vegetables and meat. Mix well and serve.

Do-ahead notes: Do up through preparation.

BOUNTIES FROM THE RIVER

The Chinese have a unique way of cooking fish so that it's both simple and flavorful. It's preferable that the fish be fresh. That's why, in Chinatown, you'll find several markets where you can choose the fish you want before it's killed. The most popular Chinese cooking method is steaming. The fish always is cooked whole because a whole fish retains juices better than one that's been cut up. You can cook any type of fish by steaming but we prefer fresh water varieties rather than salt water fish. Cook fish until JUST DONE. This way, the meat still is firm and moist. By using green onions, fresh ginger, soy sauce and hot oil, the fishy odor is reduced.

How can you tell when a fish is done? My favorite way, and an unscientific method at best, is to poke a chopstick through the meat. If it goes through easily, the fish is done. If the fish resists, it's not quite ready. If you're cooking the fish whole, the eyes will pop up and show a milky white coloring. For a more scientific approach, you'll find a 2-3 pounder takes about 25 minutes while a 1½ pounder takes about 15-20 minutes. A thicker fish requires longer cooking time; a thinner fish less.

Steamed Fish (Jing Yue)

Yield: 3–4 servings

**1 2-2½-lb. fresh or salt water fish
2 stalks green onions
3 slices fresh ginger, the size of quarters
½ tsp. salt
¼ cup salad oil
¼ cup light soy sauce**

Preparation: Shred green onions lengthwise and cut into 1-inch lengths. Sliver ginger. Clean fish, sprinkle with salt and place in a wide, shallow dish with a rim about 1-inch high.

Cooking: Place dish on steaming rack in wok. Fill bottom of wok with water. Cover. Steam fish for 20 minutes. When fish is almost done, heat ¼ cup oil in small sauce pan until sizzling hot. Take fish out of wok, pour off excess liquid. Spread green onion and ginger strips over fish. Pour hot oil over fish, then pour soy sauce over. Serve.

Do-ahead notes: Do through preparation. Never cook sea food ahead of time. It must be eaten as soon as it is cooked.

Comments: It's best to set the dish in the sink before pouring the hot oil over the fish. This way, the splattering oil will be contained in the sink. It saves cleaning up afterward.

Fish Saute with Pagoda Sauce

(Jeen Yue)

Yield: 3–4 servings

**1 2-lb. fish, either fresh or salt water
8 medium dry mushrooms, soaked for 2 hours
24 dried lily buds, soaked for 2 hours
4 tbsp. ginger root, slivered
4 cloves garlic, crushed
2 slices ginger, the size of quarters, crushed
6 tbsp. oil**

Sauce mixture:

*1 tbsp. cornstarch
1 cup chicken broth
2 tsp. sherry
2 tsp. light soy sauce
1 tsp. sesame oil*

3 green onions, shredded lengthwise, and cut into ½-inch lengths

Preparation: Stem mushrooms and cut caps into ¼-inch slices. Squeeze lily buds dry, nip off hard end and tie a knot in the middle of the bud. Prepare sauce mixture.

Cooking: Heat wok. Add 4 tbsp. oil, crushed garlic and ginger. Brown for about 1 minute. Add fish, brown on both sides, about 2-3 minutes on each side, sprinkle with salt and pepper to taste. Transfer to heated platter and keep warm. Discard ginger and garlic. Add 2 tbsp. oil to wok and heat. Add mushrooms, slivered ginger and lily buds and stir fry for 1 minute. Add sauce mixture to wok. Stir until sauce bubbles. Add fish and green onions. Baste fish with sauce and simmer for 1 minute. Transfer fish to serving platter and pour sauce over.

Do-ahead notes: Do through preparation.

Comments: You may use fillet of sole or any other fish fillets. Breading the more delicate fillet will prevent it from breaking up when sauteing. Since fish prepared this way has no fishy taste, it's a great recipe for those who claim they don't like fish. Try it! You may stop hating fish!

Jade and Coral Prawns

(Kare Jup Ha Kow)

Yield: 4 servings

1 lb. medium prawns
1 large green pepper, cut into 1-inch chunks
2 tbsp. fresh ginger root, slivered
2 cloves garlic, crushed
1 tsp. salt
1 tsp. sherry
3 tbsp. oil
Sauce mixture:
  3 tbsp. catsup
  1 tsp. sugar
  2 tsp. sherry
  1 tsp. cornstarch
  1 tbsp. light soy sauce
  3 tbsp. chicken stock

Preparation: Shell, devein and clean prawns. Blot dry. Cut along back side but don't cut through. Prepare sauce mixture.

Cooking: Heat wok. Add 1 tbsp. oil and reheat. Stir fry green pepper for 1 minute. Set aside. Add 2 tbsp. oil and crushed garlic to wok. Brown. Discard garlic. Add ginger strips with prawns and stir fry until prawns turn pink. Quickly add the sherry and salt. Stir fry for ½ minute. Add sauce mixture and stir until thickened. Add green peppers. Mix well before serving.

Do-ahead notes: Do through preparation.

Prawns in Black Bean Sauce

(See Jup Ha Kow)

Yield: 4 servings

1 lb. medium prawns
½ tsp. salt
1 green pepper, cut in 1-inch chunks
2 tbsp. salted black beans
1 clove garlic, minced
2 tbsp. fresh ginger root, minced
¼ cup chicken stock
1 tsp. cornstarch
3 tbsp. oil

Preparation: Shell, devein and clean prawns. Blot dry. Cut along back side but don't cut through. Wash and rinse black beans 2-3 times. Combine with garlic and ginger and mash together until pasty. Add stock and cornstarch. Set aside.

Cooking: Heat wok. Add 1 tbsp. oil and reheat. Stir fry green pepper for 1 minute. Set aside. Add 2 tbsp. oil to wok and heat. Stir fry prawns and salt until prawns turn pink. Add black bean mixture and stir until thickened. Add green pepper, stir and serve.

Do-ahead notes: Do through preparation.

Fried Prawns in Shells (Jeen Ha Look)

Yield: 4 servings

1 lb. prawns
2 stalks green onions
2 tbsp. fresh ginger root, slivered
2 cloves garlic, crushed
1 tsp. salt
1 tsp. light soy sauce
2 tbsp. sherry
3 tbsp. oil

Preparation: Remove legs from prawns but don't shell or remove tail. Shred green onions lengthwise and cut into 1-inch strips. Mix light soy sauce with sherry.

Cooking: Heat wok. Add 3 tbsp. oil and reheat. Add salt and garlic and brown for 1 minute. Discard garlic. Add prawns, green onions and ginger strips. Saute prawns on both sides until pink. Quickly add soy sauce mixture. Stir fry for ½ minute until all flavors are well blended. Serve.

Do-ahead notes: Do through preparation.

Comments: This is, by far, the most preferred method of cooking prawns. The shells trap the flavor of the sauce inside the prawns and, at the same time, shield them from coming into direct contact with the wok. The prawns are juicier and tastier. The correct way to eat them is to remove the shell with your teeth while sucking the sauce trapped inside. An experienced prawn-eater never will have to use his hands to remove the shell!

Deep Fried Prawns with Batter

(Jow Ha)

Yield: 4 servings

1 lb. prawns
1 tsp. salt
¾ cup flour
2 tsp. baking powder
1 cup cornstarch
1 egg
1 tbsp. oil
¾ cup water
4 cups oil

Preparation: Shell prawns, leaving tails on. Devein and clean. Sprinkle with salt and mix well. Refrigerate for two hours. Mix flour, baking powder, cornstarch, egg, oil and water to make a batter.

Cooking: Heat wok. Add 4 cups oil and reheat. Holding the prawns by the tails, dip in batter, then drop into hot oil. Fry until golden, turning once. Drain. Serve hot.

Do-ahead notes: Deep fry, cool and freeze. Preheat oven at 350°. Place frozen prawns in single layer on cookie sheet and heat for 12-15 minutes.

Comments: Use cocktail sauce, chili sauce or sweet and sour sauce for dipping. One cup prepared biscuit mix may be substituted for the flour and baking powder.

MOTHER EARTH

Crisp vegetables are a distinct characteristic of good Chinese cooking. This is one technique you must master if you aspire to become a good cook of Chinese food. Keep in mind that each vegetable has its own cooking time because of differences in texture and water content. Therefore, they must be treated individually when cooking in order to preserve their color and crispness.

Again, it is extremely important that you preheat the wok to hot before adding the oil. Then heat the oil to sizzling before adding the vegetables. If you disregard these rules, you'll end up with soggy, oily vegetables. When properly prepared, the vegetables will retain their original color and, what's more, the color usually becomes brighter. Always add a dash of sugar to the vegetables during stir frying since the sugar brings out the sweet, fresh taste.

The following charts divide vegetables into three categories — soft, medium and hard — with suggested amounts, techniques and cooking times. The last column lists vegetables which are compatible with each other should you wish to stir fry several vegetables at one time.

For instance, you may stir fry zucchini with water chestnuts and red bell pepper for a tasty combo. The colors blend well and the textures offer maximum contrast. Don't mix more than 3-4 vegetables together or the dish will look like you're trying to get rid of your leftovers.

When you're stir frying several vegetables for one dish, do each separately unless they have the same cooking time and there's enough room in the wok to accommodate both. There is no hard and fast rule governing which vegetable to stir fry first. I usually stir fry the most aromatic such as onions or celery first since the aroma will flavor the subsequent vegetables. Brown the crushed ginger and garlic only when you stir fry the last vegetable. When that's done, return everything to the wok for a quick stir to reheat. The following sample will show you how to use the chart:

Stir fry green beans with Oriental mushrooms, onions and red bell peppers.

1. Use amount of vegetables suggested in the chart.
2. Follow cutting instructions. In cases where two types of cuts are suggested (as in red bell pepper and onions) choose the cut to conform to the shape of the main vegetable, green beans in this case.
3. Stir fry onions with red bell pepper according to instructions on the chart and set aside.
4. Stir fry Oriental mushrooms according to the chart and set aside.
5. Brown crushed garlic and ginger, add green beans and stir fry according to the chart. When done, add onions, red bell peppers and mushrooms.
6. Check seasonings before serving.

Here's what to do if you want to serve meat in the same dish. Use flank steak, chicken breast or pork butt. Slice thin, across the grain. The amount is up to you but usually ranges from ½ to ¾ pound. Marinate the sliced meats for 15-30 minutes in the following marinade: 2 tsp. cornstarch, ½ tsp. sugar, 1 tsp. sherry, ½ tsp. salt and 1 tbsp. light soy sauce. Make a sauce mixture by combining 2 tsp. cornstarch, ½ cup chicken broth and 1 tsp. light soy sauce.

Now follow the cooking steps in the green bean recipe through Step 5. Set the green beans aside when done. The only other change is not to brown the crushed garlic and ginger until just before you stir fry the meat, which is the next step. When the meat is almost done, add the sauce mixture and stir until thickened. Then add vegetables, correct seasoning and serve.

By using this basic formula and trying different combinations from the chart, you can create a virtually unlimited number of dishes. The information all is here. Now it's up to you to apply it!

A GUIDE TO STIRFRYING

TYPE	NAME	MOST COMMON CUTS	AMOUNT
1. *Soft and some canned vegetables. Approximate cooking time: 1 minute.*	**BEANSPROUTS**	No cutting needed.	2 cups
	ICEBERG LETTUCE	Tears off like salad.	1 small head
	FRESH MUSHROOMS	Large—slice thin. Small—leave whole.	1-2 cups
	CANNED BUTTON MUSHROOMS	No cutting needed.	one 4 oz. can
	WATERCHESTNUTS	Quartered or sliced thin.	1 cup
	TOMATOES	Wedges.	2 small or 1 medium
2. *Medium vegetables. Cooking time approximately 2-3 minutes.*	**ASPARAGUS**	¼″ thick diagonal slices.	2-3 cups
	CANNED BAMBOO SHOOTS	Diced, chunks, or thin matchstick size strips.	1 cup

PROCEDURE 1	PROCEDURE 2	GOOD IN CONJUNCTION WITH:
Heat wok, add 2 tbsp. oil, 1 chunk crushed ginger and 1 clove garlic. Brown and discard. Add vegetable. Toss for 1 minute. Add ½ tsp. sugar and salt to taste.		celery, mushrooms, green pepper, red bell pepper, snow peas, carrots
		red bell pepper
		asparagus, peas, carrots
		all medium and hard vegetables except for bitter melon, bok choy, Oriental mushrooms, and Chinese cabbage
		canned button mushrooms and all medium and hard vegetables except for bitter melon, bok choy, Chinese cabbage, and onions
		celery, onions, green pepper, zucchini
	Add 2 tsp. water, cover for 1 minute.	beansprouts, Oriental mushrooms, red bell pepper, carrots
		fresh mushrooms, celery, Oriental mushrooms, peas, green pepper, red bell pepper, snow peas, zucchini, Chinese long beans, broccoli, carrots

TYPE	NAME	MOST COMMON CUTS	AMOUNT
2. CON'T *Medium vegetables. Cooking time approximately 2-3 minutes.*	**BITTER MELON**	¼″ thick diagonal slices.	2 cups
	BOK CHOY	½″ long diagonal slices.	3-4 cups
	CELERY	Diced, chunk, or ¼″ thin diagonal slices.	1 cup
	CHINESE CABBAGE	1″ long diagonal slices.	4-5 cups
	DRIED ORIENTAL MUSHROOMS	¼″ wide strips.	½ to 1 cup
	ONIONS	Diced or cut in wedges.	1 medium
	PEAS—FRESH OR FROZEN	No cutting necessary.	½ to 1 cup
	PEPPER—GREEN	Chunks or thin match-stick size strips.	1 medium

PROCEDURE 1	PROCEDURE 2	GOOD IN CONJUNCTION WITH:
Heat wok, add 2 tbsp. oil and 1 chunk crushed ginger and 1 clove garlic. Brown and discard. Add vegetable. Toss for 1 minute. Add ½ tsp. sugar and salt to taste.	Add 2 tsp. water, cover for 1 minute.	beansprouts, Oriental mushrooms, red bell pepper, carrots
	Add 1 tsp. water, cover for 1½ to 2 minutes.	onions, red bell peppers, carrots
	Add 1 tsp. water, toss for 1 more minute.	bamboo shoots, Oriental mushrooms, onions, peas, red bell pepper, carrots, and all soft vegetables except for iceberg lettuce
	Add 2 tbsp. water and cover for 2 minutes.	red bell pepper
	Add 1½ tsp. water, and ½ tsp. light soy sauce, cover for 1 minute.	beansprouts, water chestnuts, and all medium and hard vegetables, except for bitter melon, bok choy, and Chinese cabbage
	Add 1 tsp. water, toss for 1 minute.	mushrooms, tomatoes, asparagus, bamboo shoots, celery, peas, peppers, snow peas, zucchini, Chinese long beans, green beans, broccoli, carrots
	Add 1 tsp. water, toss for 1 minute.	canned button mushrooms, water chestnuts, bamboo shoots, Oriental mushrooms, onions, red bell peppers, carrots
	Add 1 tsp. water, toss for 1 minute.	beansprouts, mushrooms, water chestnuts, tomatoes, bamboo shoots, onions, red bell peppers, carrots

TYPE	NAME	MOST COMMON CUTS	AMOUNT
2.CON'T *Medium vegetables. Cooking time approximately 2-3 minutes.*	**PEPPER—RED BELL**	Chunks or thin match stick size strips.	1 medium
	SNOW PEAS	No cutting necessary.	2 cups
	ZUCCHINI	¼″ thick diagonal slices or ½″ rolling cut.	2 cups
3. *Hard vegetables. Approximate cooking time 3-4 minutes.*	**BEANS—CHINESE LONG**	Dice or break into 1″ length.	2-3 cups
	BEANS—GREEN	Break into 1″ length.	2-3 cups
	BROCCOLI	Flowerettes—1″ lengths. Stems—quarter, cut 1″ long.	3-4 cups
	CARROTS	⅛″ diagonal slices or thin match stick size strips.	1 cup

PROCEDURE 1	PROCEDURE 2	GOOD IN CONJUNCTION WITH:
Heat wok, add 2 tbsp. oil, 1 chunk crushed ginger and 1 clove garlic. Brown and discard. Add vegetable. Toss for 1 minute. Add ½ tsp. sugar and salt to taste.	Add 1 tsp. water, toss for 1 minute.	all types of vegetables except carrots
	Add 1 tbsp. water, toss for 1 - 2 minutes.	canned button mushrooms, water chestnuts, bamboo shoots, Oriental mushrooms, onions, red bell peppers, carrots
	For slices — same as above. Rolling cut — add 2 tsp. water, cover for 1 minute.	mushrooms, water chestnuts, tomatoes, bamboo shoots, onions, red bell peppers, carrots
	Add 2 tbsp. water, cover and cook for 2-3 minutes.	canned button mushrooms, water chestnuts, bamboo shoots, onions, red bell peppers, Oriental mushrooms
	Add 2 tbsp. water, cover and cook for 2-3 minutes.	mushrooms, water chestnuts, bamboo shoots, onions, red bell peppers, carrots
	Add 1 tsp. sugar and 2 tsp. sherry. Cover and cook for 2 minutes.	canned button mushrooms, water chestnuts, onions, red bell peppers, carrots
	Add 2 tbsp. water, cover and cook for 2-3 minutes.	beansprouts, water chestnuts, asparagus, bamboo shoots, celery, Oriental mushrooms, onions, green peppers, snow peas, zucchini, green beans, broccoli

THE GOOD OLD RELIABLES—
RICE, NOODLES AND EGGS

Why do I call them the good old reliables? Well, I don't have to explain about rice. As for noodles — everybody likes them. And the eggs — in China we always have some in the nests. If an unexpected guest drops in, you can add another dish by quickly steaming a few eggs or scrambling them with whatever vegetables you have have on hand.

RICE

Much folklore is connected with rice. For instance, it's considered a bad omen if you break a rice bowl any time of year but especially during Chinese New Year. It means you may lose your job or suffer some financial loss in the coming year because, to lose your job, is to break your rice bowl. As a child, I was taught to believe I had to finish every grain in my rice bowl because my future husband would have as many pockmarks on his face as there were grains left in the bowl.

Rice is to the Chinese what bread and potatoes are to Americans. Since rice has a bland, neutral flavor, it acts as a perfect palate-clearer in a Chinese meal particularly if two, three or more entrees are served. A small bit of rice is taken between sampling the entrees. By doing this, you clear your taste buds of one flavor so you can fully appreciate the flavor of the next dish. That's why you never should flavor the rice with salt, butter or anything else. It should be consumed "au naturel." Consequently, you can see how important it is to have plenty of rice when serving a Chinese dinner. One of the greatest mistakes a hostess can commit in serving a meal to a Chinese is to run short of rice.

This reminds me of an experience my husband and I had recently at the home of some very dear friends, a Caucasian couple. The husband had been experimenting with Chinese cooking and was anxious that we try some. He made sweet and sour pork, stir fry beef with bean sprouts and Mongolian lamb. Everything was absolutely marvelous! But, to my husband's chagrin, the host made only two cups of cooked rice for the four of us. That's not even enough for my husband alone! Consequently, we couldn't fully enjoy the dinner even though everything was delicious. When you have Chinese guests, it's far better to run out of entrees than to run out of rice!

We use two kinds of rice. Long grain, used for our daily meals, is the most common and, when properly cooked, each grain separates easily and isn't sticky. The other kind is glutinous rice, also called pearl rice or sweet rice. The Japanese call it mochigome. This rice, which has a very sticky consistency when cooked, is much shorter, rounder and has an opaque, chalk-white color. We use this for rice stuffing and for a special dish resembling the tamale.

We never use any pre-conditioned or pre-cooked rice. It has no substance; it's like biting into a puff of cotton candy. Perhaps some of you never have used anything but pre-cooked rice. Perhaps you're afraid the other kinds won't turn out. Don't be. Here's a simple recipe to follow and a 100% fail proof way to cook rice. And there's a bonus. It won't leave a brown crust at the bottom of the pan to scrub and scrub. So on to perfect rice, everytime!

Boiled Rice (Faan)

Yield: 3 cups cooked rice

1 cup raw long grain rice
1½ cups water

Preparation: Wash and rinse rice 3 times in a small sauce pan, changing the water each time. After the third rinse, drain and add 1½ cups water.

Cooking: Turn burner to high, set pan on burner and bring rice to a boil. Continue boiling, uncovered, over high heat until most (80%) of the water has evaporated and wells form on top of the rice. Cover, turn burner to the lowest setting on your stove, and continue to cook for 10 minutes. Turn burner off and let rice rest for 10 minutes before serving.

Do-ahead notes: Do through preparation.

Comments: See, I told you it's easy. You don't know how to wash rice? Simple. Pour enough water into the pan to cover rice and rub the wet rice between your hands. The washing removes the starchy film on the outer surface so the rice will be less sticky. Some of you will say I'm washing vitamins away. That may be true but you get so many vitamins from stir fry dishes, the loss of a few won't hurt.

Fried Rice Cantonese (Chow Faan)

Yield: 4–6 servings

1 egg, beaten
½ cup onion, diced
½ cup celery, diced
½ cup fresh or frozen peas
½ cup ham or barbecued pork, diced
½ cup cooked shrimp (not canned)
3 cups cold cooked rice
2 stalks green onion, diced
1-2 tbsp. dark soy sauce
1 tbsp. light soy sauce
1 tsp. salt
4 tbsp. oil

Preparation: Make certain all ingredients are diced to the same size as the peas.

Cooking: Heat wok. Add 1 tsp. oil and reheat. Stir fry egg for 20 seconds. Set aside. Add 1 tsp. oil and stir fry onions with celery for 1 minute. Set aside. Add 1 tsp. oil and stir fry peas for 1-2 minutes. Set aside. Add 1 tbsp. oil and stir fry ham and shrimp for 2 minutes. Set aside. Add 2 tbsp. oil and stir fry rice, breaking up lumps as you fry. Season with salt and stir until heated through. Add all other ingredients and season with soy sauce. Mix well and serve.

Do-ahead notes: Cook in advance and reheat, loosely covered with foil, in a 350° oven for ½ hour.

Fried Rice Singapore
(Chow Faan Singapore)

Yield: 3–4 servings

> **2 cups cooked rice, cool**
> **½ cup almond slivers**
> **½ cup raisins**
> **½ cup fresh or frozen peas**
> **½ cup red bell pepper, diced**
> **1½ tsp. salt**
> **6 tbsp. butter**

Preparation: Soak raisins ½ hour. Drain.

Cooking: Heat wok over medium heat. Add 1 tbsp. butter and stir fry almonds until golden. Set aside. Add 1 tbsp. butter and stir fry peas and red bell pepper for 2 minutes. Set aside. Add 1 tbsp. butter and stir fry raisins for 1 minute. Set aside. Add 3 tbsp. butter and stir fry rice with salt, breaking up lumps. When rice is thoroughly heated, add all other ingredients. Mix well and serve.

Do-ahead notes: Cook ahead and reheat, loosely covered with foil, in 350° oven for ½ hour.

Comments: This recipe is from my dear friend and master chef, Ken Wolfe. It's a delicious accompaniment to tomato beef curry or any curry, for that matter. Pimento may be used as a substitute for red bell pepper.

Seven Flavor Rice (Gnaw Mai Faan)

Yield: 4–5 servings

> **¾ cup long grain rice, washed**
> **¾ cup glutinous rice, washed**
> **2¼ cup water**
> **3 dried mushrooms, soaked for 2 hours**
> **4 strips bacon**
> **1 set chicken giblets (liver, heart and gizzard)**
> **½ cup onion, diced**
> **½ cup celery, diced**
> **2 stalks green onion**
> **1-2 tbsp. light soy sauce**
> **1 tsp. sesame oil**
> **½ tsp. salt**

Preparation: Stem mushrooms and dice caps fine. Cut bacon into small strips. Dice liver, heart, gizzard and green onion.

Cooking: Cook rice in 2¼ cups water according to boiled rice directions. While rice is cooking, heat wok and stir fry bacon with the giblets until done, about 3-4 minutes. Set aside. There should be some bacon fat left. If not, add 1 tbsp. oil and stir fry celery, onion and mushrooms for 2 minutes. Add meat mixture. When rice is done add, while still hot, to mixture in wok. Add salt, soy sauce, sesame oil and green onions. Mix well and serve.

Do-ahead notes: Prepare in advance and reheat, loosely covered with foil, in 350° oven for ½ hour.

NOODLES

Noodles are a great favorite with the Chinese who like to eat them for lunch or late evening snacks. We never serve noodles for dinner except on birthdays when they signify longevity. However, they can be served as part of a buffet.

Fresh egg noodles can be purchased in Chinatown grocery stores or from noodle factories.

Many supermarkets carry frozen Chinese egg noodles. Fresh Italian egg noodles are a good substitute. Although they're a bit doughier than Chinese egg noodles, they're satisfactory.

The three most popular ways of preparing noodles are: (1) in soup such as won ton soup, (2) stir fried as in chow mein, or (3) served with a sauce on top as in lo mein. All are delicious and easy to prepare.

Beef Lo Mein (Gnow Yuke Lo Main)

Yield: 2 servings

½ lb. egg noodles
½ lb. flank steak
Meat marinade:
  1 tsp. cornstarch
  1 tbsp. light soy sauce
  1 tsp. sherry
½ tsp. salt
1 clove garlic, crushed
Sauce mixture:
  1 tbsp. cornstarch
  1 cup chicken stock
  1 tbsp. light soy sauce
  2 tbsp. oyster sauce
1 tsp. sesame oil
1 stalk green onion, diced
2 tbsp. oil

Preparation: Par boil fresh egg noodles for 3 minutes. Rinse with cold water and drain. Slice beef into ⅛-inch strips across the grain. Marinate for 15 minutes. Prepare sauce mixture. Have a pot of hot water handy.

Cooking: Heat wok. Add 2 tbsp. oil and reheat. Add garlic and brown. Discard. Add beef and salt. Stir until ¾ done. Add sauce mixture and stir until thickened. Add green onions and sesame oil. Mix well and keep warm. Drop noodles in hot water. Stir for a minute to heat. Drain well. Transfer noodles to individual Chinese soup bowls. Pour meat and sauce over noodles and serve.

Do-ahead notes: Do through preparation.

Comments: Try adding different vegetable combinations along with the meat according to chart in vegetable section. If you prefer, transfer noodles to a large platter and pour meat and sauce on top ala spaghetti. Mama mia!

Barbecued Pork Chow Mein

(Char Siu Chow Mein)

Yield: 4 servings

2 cups barbecued pork, sliced thin
¾ lb. egg noodles
3 cups bok choy, sliced diagonally
¼ lb. bean sprouts
1 cup celery, sliced diagonally
1 medium onion, cut in thin wedges
1 stalk green onion, shredded lengthwise and
  cut in 1-inch pieces
4 tbsp. oil
1 tsp. sugar
1 tsp. salt
Sauce mixture:
  1 tbsp. cornstarch
  1 cup chicken stock
2 tbsp. oyster sauce
2 tsp. light soy sauce
1 tsp. sesame oil

Preparation: Par boil noodles for 3 minutes. Rinse with cold water and drain well. Line cookie sheet with foil and rub with 1 tbsp. oil. Put boiled noodles in a thin layer on cookie sheet. Place in a preheated 400° oven for 20 minutes. The noodles will stick together and form a sheet. Turn over and brown for 10 more minutes. Cool. Break into small pieces. Prepare sauce mixture. Wash and drain bean sprouts.

Cooking: Heat wok. Add 1 tbsp. oil and reheat. Stir fry onions with celery for 1 minute. Add ¼ tsp. salt and 1 tbsp. water. Cover and cook for 1 minute and set aside. Add 1 tbsp. oil and stir fry bok choy for 1 minute. Add ¼ tsp. salt and 1 tbsp. water. Cover and cook for 1 minute. Set aside. Add 1 tbsp. oil and stir fry bean sprouts for 1 minute. Set aside. Add 1 tbsp. oil and stir fry roast pork for 1 minute. Set aside.

Turn heat to medium, pour sauce mixture into wok, stirring until it begins to bubble. Add noodles, stirring and mixing until they soften. Add remaining ½ tsp. salt and 1 tsp. sugar. Add meat and stir fried vegetables, green onion, soy sauce, oyster sauce and sesame oil. Mix well and serve.

Do-ahead notes: Prepare in advance but under-cook the vegetables. Reheat, loosely covered, in slow oven for ½ hour. Make sure food is at room temperature before reheating.

Comments: THIS is authentic chow mein. Those deep-fried crispy noodles are considered an insult to the Chinese cuisine.

Won Ton Soup (Won Ton Tong)

Yield: 4 servings

>**30 won ton filled according to recipe on page 17**
>**1 cup roast pork, sliced**
>**1 qt. chicken and pork stock**
>**2 stalks green onions, minced**
>**1 tsp. sesame oil**

Preparation: Prepare won ton filling and wrap as shown on pages 17-18. Heat stock.

Cooking: Bring a pot of water to a boil. Add won ton and boil for 4-5 minutes. Remove won ton with bamboo skimmer or slotted spoon and transfer to soup bowls. Garnish with roast pork and green onions. Pour heated stock over won ton. Drizzle sesame oil over won ton and serve.

Do-ahead notes: Wrap and freeze won ton. Drop frozen won ton directly into boiling water and boil for 5-6 minutes.

Comments: Unless you're Chinese you probably don't know what won ton means. "Won" means cloud and "ton" means swallow. Since won ton wrappers are as light and fragile as clouds, biting into won ton is like swallowing a cloud.

EGGS

I love them and I hope you do, too.

Egg Foo Yung (Foo Yung Dahn)

Yield: 6–8 servings

>**6 eggs, lightly beaten**
>**¼ lb. bean sprouts**
>**¼ lb. cooked shrimp (not canned)**
>**3 strips bacon**
>**½ cup barbecued pork, diced**
>**1 2½-oz. can sliced or chopped mushrooms**
>**1 stalk green onion, minced**
>**¼ tsp. salt**

>**Sauce mixture:**
>>*1 ¾ cup chicken broth*
>>*½ tsp. salt*
>>*½ tsp. sugar*
>>*½ tsp. monosodium glutimate*
>>*2 tsp. dark soy sauce*
>>*1 ½ tbsp. cornstarch*
>>*2 tbsp. water*

>**Oil for stir frying**

Preparation: Cut bacon into thin strips. Wash and drain bean sprouts. Drain mushrooms. Prepare sauce mixture.

Cooking: Heat sauce mixture in a small pan over medium high heat. Stir until thickened and keep warm. Heat wok. Stir fry bacon with shrimp and barbecued pork and set aside. Add 1 tbsp. oil and reheat. Stir fry bean sprouts for 1 minute. Set aside.

Mix all ingredients into beaten egg.

Pour a little oil into a skillet over medium high heat. Ladle ½-¾ cup of egg mixture into the skillet. Brown on both sides. Repeat until all the egg mixture is used. Stack egg foo yung like pancakes. Pour some sauce over and serve. Pass remaining sauce around the table.

Do-ahead notes: Do through preparation. Make the sauce.

Comments: The following ingredients may be substituted:

Vegetables: bamboo shoots, chopped onions, water chestnuts, diced celery.

Meat: Chicken, crab, ham.

To make egg foo yung a uniform size, use an omelet pan or cut a 1 lb. coffee can into 1-inch high rings. Set rings on skillet and pour egg mixture inside. Don't remove rings until you're ready to brown the other side. You'll have the same size every time!

Steamed Eggs (Jing Dahn)

Yield: 4 servings

4 eggs
An equal amount of boiled, cooled water*
1 tsp. light soy sauce
¼ tsp. salt

Preparation: Beat eggs in a heat–proof dish—two cups deep (such as a Chinese soup bowl). Add water, salt and soy sauce. Mix well.

Cooking: Set dish on steaming rack in the wok. Fill bottom of wok with water. Cover. Bring water to a boil and immediately lower heat. Steam for 15 minutes or until eggs are set. Remove and drizzle with 1 tsp. light soy sauce and ½ tsp. oil. Serve.

Do-ahead notes: Eggs can be kept warm in the steamer for several hours.

Comments: The texture of steamed eggs is similar to custard. When cooked to perfection, the eggs are smooth and velvety. By using the boiled, cooled water, the texture of the eggs will be extra smooth. Care must be taken to turn down heat immediately after the water comes to a boil. Continued cooking over high heat results in a wrinkled, pourous, coarse texture. The eggs will shrivel and become most unattractive and unappetizing.

I usually use the empty egg shells to measure water.

64

WHAT'S A ROAST PIG DOING IN A CHINESE WEDDING?

Next to the New Year festivities, the Chinese wedding was, perhaps, the most noisy and colorful celebration. The entire village joined in the party which lasted until the bridegroom got drunk! But before going any further, let's go back a few months when a matchmaker began the affair.

A Chinese girl was considered marriageable when she reached 15 and, if she was at all pretty, matchmakers would call on her parents with pictures and family backgrounds of eligible males from other villages. Marriage to young men within the village was forbidden since we all had the same last name and, presumably, were all related, no matter how distantly. Marriage to anyone else with the same last name, even from another village, also was tabu for the same reason. Parents wouldn't hesitate to disown a child who broke this tradition. This unwritten law is not so rigidly observed today in the United States but, in those days, to be disowned was a painful and shameful experience. (In these days, you're lucky if the child doesn't disown you first!)

When the two families finally agreed upon their choice, they'd consult an astrologer to see if the young couple's birth signs were in harmony. If all went well, the astrologer would select the engagement and wedding dates.

The bride's family would pass out assorted cookies and cakes to all the villagers to announce the engagement. The wedding usually took place soon afterward.

During all this time the bride and groom had never met. They knew each other through pictures and information received from parents and friends. They'd really be in for a surprise if the photographer did a good touch up job!

Now came the night before the wedding. It was unbelievable. I remember one night when I was awakened by a group of women sobbing and wailing so loudly I thought someone must have died. When I found out it was coming from the bride's house I thought she must have been jilted. But my aunt told me it's customary for the bride to cry all night to show her parents how much she loved them and how much she hated to leave them. Her close friends usually joined in for moral and vocal support. The louder the racket, the happier her parents!

The next day the bride was dressed entirely in red (not white, since that is the color of mourning in China). She wore a floor length gown with matching jacket and an elegantly elaborate headdress decorated with sequins, pearls and gold flowers. She was completely covered and a red veil hid her face. (Thank goodness for the veil. After all that crying the night before her nose must have been as red as Rudolph's and her eyes must have looked like road maps. And it's a good thing she didn't have to say anything. All that wailing certainly must have given her a good case of laryngitis.)

By this time, the bamboo sedan chair sent by the groom arrived. Carried by two men, it was no larger than a telephone booth with a seat inside for one passenger. There were no bridesmaids. Only her immediate relatives, her trousseau and at least one roast pig made the journey to the bridegroom's house. If the family could afford it, there were more roast pigs.

All the people in the bridegrooms's village welcomed the bride and tried to get a glimpse of her. When she stepped down from the sedan chair, firecrackers went off and musicians played joyous melodies. The bride was ushered inside the house, the marriage ceremony was performed by the village elder, and all the relatives plus anyone else who could squeeze in witnessed the rites.

The bride's first duty, immediately afterwards, was to pay respects to her in-laws by performing the tea ceremony. With much humbleness, she would bow to each of her in-laws and other family elders while holding a tray with filled tea cups on it. In a tiny, tiny voice (in some cases it must have been a hoarse whisper depending on the amount of crying the night before), she addressed them by their titles. In return, she was given jewelry or money to show how much she was welcomed. It was not uncommon for the tea ceremony to last several hours since she might have to bow to 40 or 50 people. By this time, she was so loaded with jewelry and money she looked like a walking Christmas tree with all the trimmings. This ancient ritual still is an integral part of Chinese wedding ceremony in this country.

The banquet was served after the tea ceremony. Thank goodness the bride finally had a chance to sit down.

When it was time to retire, the family would pile food on the bridal bed and, at a given signal, all the kids would jump on the bed and grab the food. The idea was that, hopefully, the couple would produce as many children as there were those who jumped onto the bed.

The roast pig, brought by the bride, was not consumed during the banquet because . . . ahem, if the bride was not as pure as the day she was born, back she went in the sedan chair along with her trousseau and the *uneaten* roast pig!

The young bride's primary duty was to look after the comforts of her mother-in-law, father-in-law and husband. She had no say whatsoever in running the household and she had to do as she was told by all the family elders. (No wonder she cried so much the night before the wedding.)

A wealthy man could have one or more concubines. Often, if she had produced no sons, this was at the urging of his wife. This was because a man's life was considered incomplete if he didn't have at least one son to carry on the family name.

Concubines had the status of common-law wives and their male offspring were on an equal with the wife in matters of inheritance. But the wife usually didn't mind the concubines because she was their boss and they waited on her hand and foot. My mother's father had three concubines and my grandmother never had it so good!

Roast Suckling Pig

1 20—25 lb. Suckling Pig

Marinade for Pig
½ cup hoisin sauce
½ cup bean sauce
6 tbsp. salt
4 tbsp. sherry, brandy or rice wine
2 tbsp. 5 spice powder
1 whole bulb minced garlic

½ cup honey
½ cup dark soy sauce
¼ cup bacon drippings

Preparation: Rub marinade mixture into the piglet's cavity and lay it on its back overnight in the refrigerator. Before roasting, redistribute the marinade in the cavity by rubbing it again.

Using wood from a vegetable crate, saw off 2 or 3 pieces which would just fit crosswise into the interior of the cavity. Wrap the wooden sticks with foil and place them in the cavity so the stomach portion will fill out properly. (This is to avoid the caved-in look.) Wrap the ears and tail with foil to prevent over browning. You may even have to wrap the feet, midway during roasting, if they appear to be browning too rapidly.

Place the piglet on a roasting rack, spreading the legs apart and prop the mouth open with another small piece of wood wrapped in foil.

Roasting: Preheat oven at 450°. Place rack with piglet on roasting pan and set in the middle level of oven.

Roast piglet for 20 minutes. Turn oven to 350° and roast for about 2 to 2¼ hours. You may baste the skin with a mixture of honey, dark soy, and bacon drippings during the last 30 minutes at 10 minute intervals if you feel additional browning is necessary. Otherwise, you may omit this procedure. To give the skin a high gloss; just brush with oil at the end of roasting.

A good sign that the piglet is done is when its nose has a discharge. (This is the brain tissue.)

Comments: A true suckling pig should be 25 pounds or less. Anything bigger is most likely a young piglet which is still very good and tender. However, you may have difficulty fitting one in your oven. As a matter of fact, a 25 pounder may require a commercial size oven to do a proper job.

If you want a blister effect on the skin, you may prick the skin with a fork and then sprinkle salt on on the skin; the salt will cause the skin to blister. When roasted properly, the meat is very tender and tasty and the skin is very crispy and has a rich, deep reddish-brown appearance.

RED EGGS & GINGER

A new mother was confined to the house for an entire month, provided the family could afford help. She wasn't allowed to drink anything cold or eat any fresh fruits or vegetables during this time. The only things she could eat were salted or cured meats and vegetables. As if that weren't enough, she had to drink a thick, heavy, pickled broth made of black vinegar, ginger and pigs' feet. The vinegar broth was supposed to help the mother produce more milk for her baby. She also drank another concoction called "mother's brew." This was a chicken broth made with, among other things, wood fungus, dried lily buds, ginger root, peanuts, pieces of chicken and a *generous* amount of rice wine or whiskey. This was supposed to revitalize her and strengthen the new mother's health. For me, it had a most disasterous effect. I have zero tolerance for alcohol and this was the l-o-n-g-e-s-t cocktail party I'd ever attended!

Mother's Brew (Gai Jow)

Yield: 4–5 quarts

- 2 3-lb. fryers, chopped into 2-inch pieces
- 12 dried mushrooms, soaked for 1 hour
- 2 doz. dried lily buds, soaked for 1 hour
- 1½ cup dried wood fungus (moak yee) soaked overnight
- 6-8 dried red dates
- ¾ cup raw peanuts, shelled
- 2 chunks crushed fresh ginger roots, silver dollar size
- 4 qts. water
- 1 to 1½ cup whiskey or rice wine
- 2 tsp. sugar
- salt to taste
- 3 tbsp. oil

Preparation: Squeeze mushrooms dry. Discard stems and cut caps into ½-inch wide slices. Clean wood fungus by removing hard particles and pinch off stems. Tie each lily bud into a knot and pinch off tough end.

Cooking: Heat 3 tbsp. oil in wok. Brown crushed ginger chunks with chicken pieces then transfer to a soup pot. Next, brown lily buds, mushrooms and wood fungus. Set aside. Add red dates and raw peanuts to soup pot, cover ingredients with water and bring to a boil. Turn heat to medium for 45 minutes. Add lily buds, mushrooms, wood fungus. Simmer for 20 more minutes. Add 2 tsp. sugar and salt to taste. Just before serving, add the whiskey or rice wine.

Do-ahead notes: Cook this the day before. It tastes better after a day or two.

Comments: According to our customs, the mother's brew has certain medicinal value when taken by women who have just given birth. It is supposed to revitalize the new mother's system and chases away the "after birth blues." But you don't have to be a new mother to enjoy it.

In China, a baby was considered to be a year old the day he was born. (I won't argue with that since he was in the mother's womb for nine months.) When the New Year arrived, he was considered another year older. This was fine if his actual birthday was in January or February. But take my case. I was born on December 15th and 16 days later I was two years old. It didn't matter that much when I was in my teens but now it's an entirely different story.

The baby had his "coming out" party when he was a month old. At that time his parents invited all their friends and relatives to come over so they could show off their pride and joy. The baby was showered with gifts, money and jewelry and the guests were given dyed red eggs and pickled ginger to take home.

This was the biggest and, usually, the only birthday party he'd have until he became 60. We always revered our elders and looked to them for guidance and words of wisdom. Now, at 60, he finally had earned his undisputed place in the family and, in the winter of his life, he enjoyed the fruits of his labors. We had a great deal of respect for our elders as they approached 60, 70, 80 and 90. So, the older he got, the bigger the party.

The traditional dish served before any birthday banquet was sub gum noodles in chicken broth. Noodles were important because, being so long, they symbolized longevity. Here then, is the longevity noodle recipe for your next birthday party.

Sub Gum Noodles

Yield: 10 servings

> **1 lb. egg noodles**
> **½ lb. pork butt**
> **12 prawns**
> **6 dried mushrooms, soaked 2 hours**
> **1 cup sliced canned abalone**
> **2 cups bok choy**
> **6 cups chicken and pork stock**
> **1 tsp. sesame oil**

Preparation: Par boil noodles for 3 minutes. Rinse under cold water and drain well. Stem mushrooms and slice caps into ⅛-inch strips. Slice pork butt into ⅛-inch slices, diagonally cut bok choy into ½-inch pices. Shell, devein and clean prawns. Slice each along the center back into halves.

Cooking: Bring broth to a boil. Add sliced pork and mushrooms and cook for 1 minute. Add prawns and bok choy and cook for 2 more minutes. Add abalone and cook for 1 minute. Finally, add noodles and heat through. Stir in sesame oil. Ladle into soup bowls and serve.

Do-ahead notes: Do through preparation.

Comments: The most sub gum noodles anyone will eat at a banquet is one small bowl since it's served as a first course before the dinner proper. If you wish to serve this as a luncheon dish, use ¼ lb. of noodles per person.

THE GRAND FINALE & A NEW BEGINNING

The arrival of the New Year was the festivity we looked forward to with the greatest anticipation and celebrated with the most fanfare. It was the biggest and longest celebration of the year and usually lasted three weeks. Just imagine, if you will, putting all the important American holidays — July 4, Easter, Halloween, Thanksgiving, Christmas and New Year — together in one celebration and you'll get an idea of what our New Year celebration was like.

THE KITCHEN GOD

Each Chinese kitchen had a picture of a kitchen god pasted next to the stove. This kindly old gentleman would oversee the welfare of the family. A week before the arrival of each New Year, he was to report on the family's activities to the god in heaven. (Please, only what went on in the kitchen!) We'd burn his picture along with paper chariots and food offerings to aid his journey when he was due to report in heaven. And, to ensure a good report, we'd smear his face with syrup, honey, molasses or anything sugary so he'd have nothing but sweet things to say about us. We'd welcome him back when the New Year arrived by pasting a new picture in the kitchen.

We'd celebrate New Year's Eve with a big family dinner, not unlike the American Thanksgiving. Relatives would arrive from near and far. The housewife was busy all week preparing for this meal as well as the New Year's Day meal. All preparation had to be made in advance since she wasn't allowed to use anything sharp, such as a cleaver, on New Year's Day. Also, we couldn't eat any kind of meat on New Year's Day since we didn't want to take any life on that day. Instead, we ate a traditional Buddhist vegetarian dish called lo-hon-jai. We'd spend the day with family, just as in the Western Christmas, and we'd wear new clothes, similar to new Easter outfits.

Lo Hon Jai

Yield: 3–4 quarts

1 1-lb. can bamboo shoots, cut into thin strips
6-8 dried oysters, cleaned and soaked overnight. Reserve liquid.
6-8 dried bean curd sheets, soaked 2 hours
24 dried lily buds, soaked 1 hour
½ cup dried cloud ear fungus, soaked ½ hour
6-8 dried mushrooms, soaked 2 hours
4 oz. long rice (or bean thread), cut into 4-inch lengths, soaked in hot water for ½ hour and drained

12 fried bean curds, rinsed in hot water, squeezed dry
24 ginko nuts, shelled and soaked in boiling water for 5-10 minutes
5 cups shredded Chinese cabbage
1¾ cups chicken broth
3½ cups water
4-5 tbsp. oyster sauce
2-3 tbsp. dark soy sauce
1-2 tsp. salt (to taste)
5 tbsp. oil

Preparation: Clean, squeeze dry or drain all soaked ingredients. Peel the red membrane from ginko nuts. Nip off the tough end of the lily buds and tie a knot in the middle. Cut bean curd sheets into ½-inch lengths. Stem mushrooms and cut caps into thin strips. Dice oysters and cut fried bean curds in half.

Cooking: Heat wok. Add 1 tbsp. oil. Stir fry lily buds with cloud ear fungus for 1 minute. Set aside. Add 2 tbsp. oil and stir fry Chinese cabbage for 2-3 minutes. Set aside. Add 2 tbsp. oil and stir fry oysters, mushrooms, ginko nuts and bamboo shoots for 2 minutes. Add chicken broth, water and liquid from soaked oysters. Cover and simmer for 45 minutes. Add fried bean curd and cook for 10 minutes. Add dried bean curd sheets, cloud ear fungus, lily buds and cook 10 more minutes. Add long rice and cabbage and cook 15 minutes. Add seasoning and mix well.

Do-ahead notes: This dish freezes beautifully. It also will keep well in the refrigerator for several days. The taste improves each day.

SWEET SNACKS

The second day of our New Year was called "hoy-nin," the opening of the year. For two weeks we called on friends and relatives and, since we believed we never should visit empty handed, we'd always bring sweets as presents. I remember most vividly the sweet crescents, sesame and butterfly cookies, steamed sponge cakes and, always, Chinese white chop chicken. "Gut," or Chinese tangerines, always were brought with the other food because the word also means luck. So, with the tangerines, you also are bringing luck with your gifts.

You never were allowed to leave empty handed. The hostess always insisted you return home with half of what you brought along with some of her own goodies plus, of course, the "gut." So, you can see, for two weeks it's one, long eating orgy.

Sweet Crescents

Yield: 8–10 dozen

> ½ **cup chopped salted cocktail peanuts**
> ½ **cup coconut flakes**
> ½ **cup brown sugar**
> ½ **cup granulated sugar**
> 1 **pkg. won ton wrappers**
> 1 **egg, beaten**

Preparation: Mix peanuts, coconut, brown sugar and granulated sugar. Fold won ton squares into triangles. Round off the top corner with scissors. Place 1 tsp. filling in center. Moisten edges with beaten egg and seal.

Cooking: Deep fry in hot oil until golden, turning once. Drain. Cool. Store in air-tight container.

Do-ahead notes: These will keep for 3-4 weeks in an air-tight container.

Comments: Serve crescents as dessert with ice cream or sherbet.

Steamed Sponge Cake

Yield: 1 7-inch square or 1 9-inch round cake

> 5 **extra large eggs at room temperature**
> 1 **tbsp. water**
> 1 **cup sugar**
> 1 **cup cake flour***
> 1 **tbsp. melted butter**

Preparation: Beat eggs, water and sugar for 10 minutes at high speed or for 20 minutes by hand. The color should turn almost vanilla and the consistency becomes thick and creamy. Fold in flour, then melted butter. Line bottom of a 9-inch round or 7-inch square baking pan with cooking parchment paper. Pour batter into pan.

Cooking: Have water in wok boiling. Set cake pan on the steaming rack and cover. Steam 20 minutes at medium heat. Insert tooth pick to see if done. Turn cake out and peel off paper. Serve warm or cold.

Do-ahead notes: Cake can be stored for 2-3 days in a cake keeper.

Comments: Since this cake is served without any frosting or topping, it's appealing to those who don't like too-sweet desserts. The texture is fine and firm but not hard. When pressed down, the cake springs back like a sponge.

*Swansdown. This is the only flour available that's close to Chinese rice flour. Don't substitute any other kind.

Sesame Cookies

Yield: 10 dozen

> ½ **cup granulated sugar**
> ½ **cup brown sugar**
> **1 egg**
> ½ **lb. lard, no substitute**
> ½ **tsp. almond extract**
> **2 cups flour**
> ½ **tsp. baking soda**
> ¾ **tsp. baking powder**
> **sesame seeds**

Preparation: Sift flour with baking soda and baking powder. Cream egg and lard together. Add sugars, then almond extract. Gradually add the dry ingredients and mix well. Roll 1 tsp. dough in your hands to form a ball. Then roll in sesame seeds, coating all sides.

Cooking: Place sesame balls about ¾-inch apart on cookie sheets. Bake in pre-heated 350° oven for 8-10 minutes. Cool.

Do-ahead notes: These keep for weeks in air-tight containers.

Comments: The recipe for almond cookies is basically the same. Roll 1 tbsp. dough to make the ball, then press an almond in the middle. Brush with beaten egg yolk and bake 8-10 minutes.

Butterfly Cookies

Yield: About 80

> **1 pkg. won ton wrappers**
> **1 cup powdered sugar**
> **Oil for deep frying**

Preparation: Cut each won ton wrapper into 2 rectangles. Lay one rectangle on top of the other to

form a double thickness. Make three ½-inch slits in the center, lengthwise. To form a bow, pull one end through the middle slit.

Cooking: Deep fry butterflies until golden, about 1 minute or less. Drain on paper towel. Sift powdered sugar over both sides. Cool.

Do-ahead notes: These keep for several weeks in air-tight containers.

Comments: These also can be made from egg roll wrappers but they're three times as large. I prefer using won ton wrappers because I think their mini size makes them more attractive.

"LEE SEE" AND OMENS

As kids, we particularly liked the "lee see" tradition. Lee sees are red packets with money inside given only to children and unmarried adults by married people. To receive the lee see (which means smooth affairs in Chinese), the children had to bow to the elders and say "gong hay fat choy" or "I wish you a prosperous New Year." Abracadabra! The lee see would appear like magic! It's much like the trick or treat tradition here. But Chinese children were more naive. They hadn't thought of the trick part.

This was the only time Chinese kids received money since there was no such thing as an allowance. The lee see had to last for spending money until the next year.

Because the Chinese are very superstitious, no one is allowed to say one harsh word let alone quarrel or fight, during the entire New Year celebration. We kids had to be on our best behavior for at least two full weeks. But watch out afterwards! All hell could break loose!

All debts had to be paid by midnight on New Year's Eve. Thank goodness credit cards weren't available. You couldn't break a rice bowl or drop a chop stick because that meant the head of the household might lose his job. If we did break a rice bowl or drop a chop stick, we'd say "dai gut lee see," the equivalent of saying "God bless you" when someone sneezes here.

The seventh day of the New Year was called "yun yut" or "little people's day." The kids would be served a plain bowl of thick rice soup (joak) with a long green onion stem. Since green onions grow long, straight and without knots, it was the hope of the parents that their children would be smart in school and, like the green onion, without any knots in their heads.

THE LION DANCE

In China, the lion symbolized life, luck and virility. So, during the New Year, troupes of talented acrobats would do the lion's dance at homes and business establishments. The lion's headdress was beautifully decorated and had a long, multi-colored silk and brocade train. The head was held by one dancer and the train by another.

I can remember as a child in Hong Kong that some of these dancers could climb a pole several stories high (without benefit of safety nets) while still dancing to the beatings of the cymbals, gongs and drums. We'd hang money on a string to entice the lion who'd come and dance for us, thereby bringing us good luck. At the end of each dance, while the lion took the money, firecrackers would be set off to make sure all evil spirits were frightened away. During those two weeks, firecrackers were set off as frequently as during the July Fourth celebration here.

In the midst of all the festivities, we'd set aside one day to pay our respects to the deceased. We visited our ancestors' graves offering food and burning candles, incense, paper money, paper

clothing and other paper cut outs representing human comforts. This was to make certain our departed ones were well taken care of in the after-world.

FESTIVAL OF LIGHTS

The climax of the New Year came on the 15th day, the light festival. This celebration would welcome the advent of spring and longer days. Lanterns of all sizes, shapes and colors would be strung outside our houses, much like Christmas lights, and the dragon parade officially would end the New Year celebration.

My mother would breathe a sigh of relief after all the cooking, visiting and entertaining while the kids' pockets were filled with lee see and our heads were filled with plans to spend it. The men would look forward to a year of good crops and prosperous business affairs and, most likely, everyone gained a few pounds.

GLOSSARY OF INGREDIENTS

Here is a list of ingredients common in Chinese cooking. For the sake of simplicity, the list includes only those ingredients used in this book. All of them can be purchased from stores specializing in Oriental foods although, with the increasing interest in Chinese cooking, some now are available in supermarkets.

ANISE, STAR: (see star anise).

BAMBOO SHOOTS: An ivory-colored vegetable, usually available in cans either whole or sliced. The unused portions can be kept for about one week in jars provided you change the water each day to keep them from spoiling. (juk soon)

BEAN CAKE: Also called tofu or dow fu. Because it's made from soy beans, bean cake has a high protein content. It's an excellent food for babies since it digests easily. It's also good for children who don't care for meat.

    The bean cake has a smooth, creamy texture and a bland taste so it readily absorbs the flavor of soups and sauces. It can be purchased fresh in produce sections or it also is available in cans. Fresh bean cake spoils easily so it must be used within one or two days of purchase.

BEAN CURD STICK (DRIED): Made of the dried skin of soy bean milk. It has a glossy, creamy appearance and a chewy texture. It must be soaked before using and often is found in soups and vegetarian dishes. (fu juk)

BEAN CURD (FRIED): Another form of bean curd which has been deep fried. (dow fu kok)

BEAN SAUCE: Also called brown bean sauce. The Chinese name is "mein see." This is prepared from the residue left after making soy sauce. It has a thick consistency and is available in cans or jars. Bean sauce is used to flavor pork and fowl in addition to bland vegetables such as bean cakes. The unused portion will keep for months when stored in a jar in the refrigerator.

BEAN SPROUTS: A vegetable grown from green mung peas. It has a 2-inch long white shoot with a small green hood. The texture is delicate and crunchy. Bean sprouts shouldn't be cooked for more than a minute or they'll become limp and lose their crispness. Fresh bean sprouts don't keep well and should be used as soon as possible. (dow nga)

BEAN THREAD: Also called long rice or cellophane noodles. Chinese name is "fun see." These are dry, thin, white noodles made from ground mung peas. They puff up immediately when dropped in hot oil. They must be soaked first, however, for all other types of cooking. When cooked, the noodles become transparent: thus, cellophane noodles.

BITTER MELON: Also known as balsam pear, the Chinese name is "foo gwa." This is a green vegetable, about the size of a cucumber, with shiny, pebbly skin. Its cool and bitter taste is due to its quinine content. It shouldn't be peeled but the pulp and seeds must be scooped out before cooking. It can be sliced for stir frying or halved for stuffing. Black bean sauce is the usual flavoring.

BLACK BEANS: The Chinese name is "dow see." These are tiny, soft, extremely salty black beans. Used to season meat and seafood, they're first washed, then mashed with fresh garlic and ginger. They can be stored at room temperature.

BOK CHOY: A leafy vegetable with white stalks and dark green leaves. It looks somewhat like Swiss chard but the taste isn't as strong. Bok Choy can be stir fried alone or with meat and can be dropped into broth for soup.

CHINESE BROCOLLI: Similar in color to Western brocolli but longer and leafier. The flowers are white. When stir frying, add about 1½ tsp. sugar and 2 tbsp. sherry plus salt to enhance the flavor. (guy lang)

81

CHINESE MUSTARD POWDER: Yellow mustard powder is available in Chinese grocery stores. Mix the powder with sufficient water to form a medium thick paste. Add vinegar to enhance the hot flavor. A small amount of salad oil will give the prepared mustard a shiny appearance. Mix only the amount you plan to use. Store the powder in your pantry. (guy lut)

CHINESE PARSLEY: Also known as cilentro or coriander. This is a bright green herb with slender, delicate stems and small, serrated flat leaves. Highly aromatic, it has a strong, pungent flavor and is used as a garnish or as a bouquet in roasting poultry. (yuen sai)

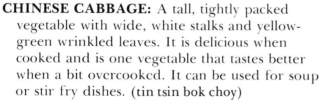

CHINESE CABBAGE: A tall, tightly packed vegetable with wide, white stalks and yellow-green wrinkled leaves. It is delicious when cooked and is one vegetable that tastes better when a bit overcooked. It can be used for soup or stir fry dishes. (tin tsin bok choy)

CHINESE SAUSAGE: The Chinese name is "lop cheung." These slender pork sausages come in pairs, each one six inches long. They're sliced thin and can be cooked directly on top of rice or steamed separately. Stir fry them with any vegetable or use in rice stuffings. To store, wrap in plastic bags and freeze.

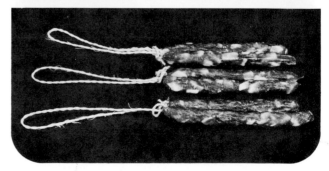

莞茜 雲耳 莞茜 豆腐 春卷皮 五香粉

CILENTRO: See Chinese parsley.

CLOUD EAR FUNGUS: A small, dried, grayish-brown fungus about one inch long. When soaked, it expands to several times its size. The texture is crunchy and delicate and it either is steamed or used in stir fried dishes (wan yee)

CORIANDER: See Chinese parsley.

DOW FU: See bean cake.

EGG ROLL WRAPPERS: Made with flour, eggs, and water, these can be purchased in Chinatown noodle factories or in the frozen food section of many supermarkets. Immediately rewrap the unused portion in plastic wrap and freeze. (chun pay)

FIVE SPICE POWDER: A blend, in powder form, of star anise, cinnamon, cloves, fennel and anise pepper. It has a mustard color and is used in roasting meats and poultry. (eng hung fun)

FUZZY MELON: Known as "mo gwa" or "jit gwa" in Chinese. This is a green vegetable about six inches long and two inches in diameter. Its skin, which must be peeled before using, is covered with a fine, white fuzz. Very tasty in soup or stir fried with meat.

GINGER, FRESH GINGER ROOT: A gnarled, spicy, beige-colored root. It's a must in Chinese cooking but ginger powder never should be substituted for it. In fact, it's better to leave it out completely if you don't have the root on hand. It's especially good to use ginger on seafood since it alleviates the fishy odor. It will keep for months if you break it into small chunks and store in a refrigerated jar filled with sherry. And wait 'til you taste that sherry! **(geung)**

GINGER, SWEET MIXED: Also known as "sub gum geung" or "sub gum" vegetables, this is canned or jarred sweet and sour ginger mixed with vegetables. It can be used as a garnish or chilled and eaten as a relish. Use the juice in place of vinegar when making sweet and sour sauce and discover the taste difference.

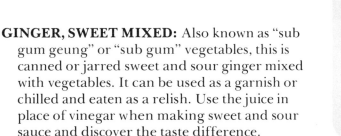

GINKO NUTS: Small, beige, hard-shelled nuts with beige meat covered with a thin red membrane. After shelling, the nuts must be soaked in boiling water for 5-10 minutes so the membrane can be peeled off. (bok guoy)

HOISIN SAUCE: A deep brownish-red sauce made from soy beans, chili, garlic and vinegar. Very thick, spicy and sweet, it's used in seasoning spareribs, roasting poultry and as a condiment, particularly with Peking duck. (hoisin cheung)

JUJUBE NUT: See red dates, dried.

LICHEE: This fruit has a red, strawberry-like skin with a white, translucent, juicy, sweet pulp. It's available in cans and is delicious when chilled. (lichee)

LILY BUDS, DRIED: The Chinese name is "gum jum." A dried, 2-inch long flower, burnished gold in color. They must be soaked and knotted to keep from falling apart during cooking. The small, hard lump at the end of each stem should be removed. They add a delicate, subtle flavor to poultry and often are used in vegetarian dishes.

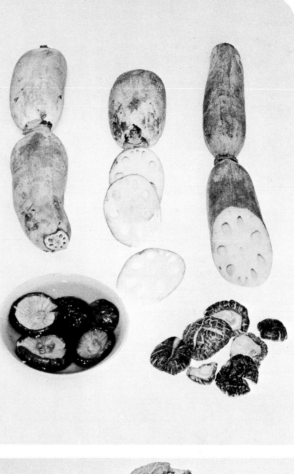

LONG RICE: See bean thread.

LOTUS ROOT: The stem of the water lily, reddish-brown in color. Two or three sections, each about six to eight inches long and two inches in diameter, are linked together like sausages to form a whole root. About five to seven tunnels run the length of each section forming interesting patterns when cut diagonally. The texture is crispy. Lotus root can be sliced thin for stir frying or sliced in ¼-inch pieces for soups. It also is available in cans. (lin gnau)

MUSHROOMS, DRIED CHINESE: These come in several grades with the best grade called "fa goo." They are thick and light in color on the underside while the surfaces of the caps have many cracks. The edges are curled. When purchased by weight, you can be sure every fa goo is almost uniform in size. Fa goo should be saved for special dishes in which mushrooms are cooked whole. For other uses, buy less expensive grades since size uniformity is inconsequential when the recipe calls for slicing or dicing. They must be soaked until soft, the stems discarded and the caps cut according to directions. No matter how poor the Chinese families may be they always discard the stems.

MUSTARD GREENS: A jade green vegetable with a thick stem and wide, curved leaves. It's slightly cool and bitter to the taste. Excellent for soup and is a favorite pickling vegetable. (guy choy)

MUSTARD POWDER, CHINESE: See Chinese Mustard Powder.

OYSTERS, DRIED: Reddish brown in color, they have a strong flavor. They should be soaked over night and cleaned well to get rid of sand between the folds. Good in soup or stir fry dishes. (ho see)

OYSTER SAUCE: A thick, rich, brown sauce made from oysters but without a strong fishy odor. Its consistency is much like catsup. It's a favorite seasoning for meat but also is used as a condiment, especially with white chop chicken. (ho mei cheung)

PICKLED MUSTARD: See turnips, Szechwan.

PLUM SAUCE: A thick, amber sauce with a pungent, spicy flavor, it's made from plums, apricots, vinegar and sugar. This chutney-like sauce is used as one of the condiments for Peking duck and also is called duck sauce. It can be stored for months, refrigerated, in a tightly-covered jar. (sheung moy cheung)

RED DATES, DRIED: Also known as jujube nuts, these are small, dried, red fruits with wrinkled, glossy skins. Used in soups or in steamed dishes to impart a subtle sweetness. (hung jut)

SAUSAGE, CHINESE: See Chinese sausage.

SESAME OIL: A strong oil with a nut-like flavor. It's never used for cooking although a half teaspoon sprinkled on top will do wonders for any dish. (mar yau)

SOY SAUCE: A thin, brown sauce made from soy beans, wheat, yeast and salt. There are two kinds: (1) Light or thin. Lighter in color and density, it's used as a condiment or in cooking dishes in which the color of the sauce shouldn't show as in seafood. (2) Dark, thick or black. This soy sauce is darker, thicker and has a full-bodied flavor. It's used when a deep brown color is desired. (sang chau see yau)

SNOW PEAS: The light green pea pod is so delicate and tender it needn't be shelled. Be sure to string them and break off the tip before using. (ho lang dow)

STAR ANISE: A small cluster of dark brown, dry seeds shaped like an 8-pointed flower. It has a strong licorice flavor and is used in making soy sauce chicken, stewing beef and in some soups. (but kok)

SWEET CUCUMBERS: See tea melons.

SWEET MIXED GINGER: See ginger, sweet mixed.

TANGERINE PEEL, DRIED: The dark brown, dried peel has a bittersweet flavor that lends subtlety to soups and poultry dishes. Always soak before using. (guoy pay)

TEA MELON: Also known as sweet cucumbers. Chinese name is "cha gwa." Amber color cucumber-like squash preserved in a syrup of honey and spices. The tiny squash is only 2 to 3 inches long and is sweet in flavor and crunchy in texture. Use chopped melons as condiment for joak—the thick Chinese rice soup, or slice them to steam with pork dishes. The tea melons are available in cans. After it is opened, store in a jar and refrigerate. They will keep for months.

TOFU: See bean cake.

TURNIP, CHINESE: Known as "lo-bak" in Chinese or "daikon" in Japanese. Daikon often is more readily available than lo-bak. This white vegetable looks like an over grown horseradish. It has a subtle flavor but exudes a very strong odor while cooking. Good for soups.

TURNIP, SALTED: Brown, with a salty flavor, these turnips can be used sparingly in meat dishes in place of salt. Adds flavor and textural interest. (law bok goue)

TURNIP, SZECHWAN: Also known as pickled mustard, this hot, peppery, canned turnip is preserved with Szechwan pepper. Use in steamed dishes and sour and hot soup. (jar choy)

WATER CHESTNUTS: A bulb-like vegetable, the size of a strawberry, grown in water. The fresh ones are covered with mud and must be washed and peeled before eating. Yes, you can eat them raw. They're delicious! Crunchy and sweet, they're also available in cans. Good for stir frying when sliced or use in meat stuffings when minced. (mar tai)

 WINTER MELON: A large, round melon with a tough, frosty, green skin and delicate white meat. They can be purchased whole or by the pound. To prepare, peel off skin, scoop out seeds and cut meat according to recipe directions. (tung guar)

 **WON TON WRAPPERS:** Made with flour, eggs and water, these can be purchased in Chinatown noodle factories or in some supermarket frozen food sections. Immediately rewrap unused portion with plastic wrap and freeze. (won ton pay)

 WOOD FUNGUS: (mook yee) A dry fungus similar to cloud ear fungus but thicker, tougher and crisper in texture. Must be soaked before using.

INDEX OF RECIPES

Meat:

BEEF:
Beef Asparagus, 44
Ginger Beef, 42
Oyster Sauce Beef, 42
Skewer Beef, 43
Steak Balls, 44
Tomato Beef Curry, 43

PORK:
Barbecued Pork, 38
Barbecued Spareribs, 38
Dow Fu and Pork in
    Bean Sauce, 39-40
Steamed Chinese Pork
    Sausages, 40
Steamed Minced Pork with
    Water Chestnuts, 39
Steamed Spareribs with
    Black Bean Sauce, 38-39
Sweet and Sour Pork, 40

CHICKEN:
Chicken Medallion with
    Snow Peas, 35
Chicken Cashew, 35-36
Coriander Chicken Salad,
    33-34
Five Spice Game Hens, 36
Plum Sauce Chicken, 31-32
Sesame Chicken, 32
Soy Sauce Chicken, 32
Soy Sauce Chicken Wings, 32
Steamed Chicken with
    Mushrooms and
    Lily Buds, 33
White Chop Chicken, 31

Noodles:

Barbecued Pork Chow
    Mein, 62
Beef Lo Mein, 62
Breakfast Noodles, 13
Sub Gum Noodles, 72
Won Ton Soup, 63

Rice:

Boiled Rice, 59
Fried Rice Cantonese, 59
Fried Rice Singapore, 60
Joak, 12-13
Seven Flavor Rice, 60

Soup:

Basic Chicken Stock, 23-24
Basic Chicken and Pork
    Stock, 24
Chinese Cabbage Soup, 25
Fuzzy Melon Soup, 25
Mongolian Hot Pot, 27-28
Mother's Brew, 69
Peas and Egg Drop Soup, 25
Sour and Hot Soup, 26-27
Turnip and Oxtail Soup, 26
Watercress and Water
    Chestnut Soup, 25
Winter Melon Soup, Village
    Style, 26
Won Ton Soup, 63

Vegetarian Dish:

Lo Hon Jai, 74

OTHER BOOKS BY TAYLOR & NG:

HERBCRAFT
WOKCRAFT
PLANTCRAFT
EGGCRAFT
BREADCRAFT
TEACRAFT
RICECRAFT